creature |the brief|

the LA+ CREATURE design ideas competition asked designers to:

• choose a nonhuman creature as a client (any species, any size, anywhere) and identify its needs (energy, shelter, procreation, movement, interaction, environment, etc).

• design (or redesign) a place, structure, thing, system, or process that improves the creature's life.

• contribute, through the design, to increasing human awareness of and empathy for the creature's existence.

Results within

IN THIS ISSUE

Endpapers: "The Entry of the Animals into
Noah's Ark" (1613) by Jan Breughel the Elder,
public domain via Wikimedia Commons.

Editorial: Image by Ian Dillon.

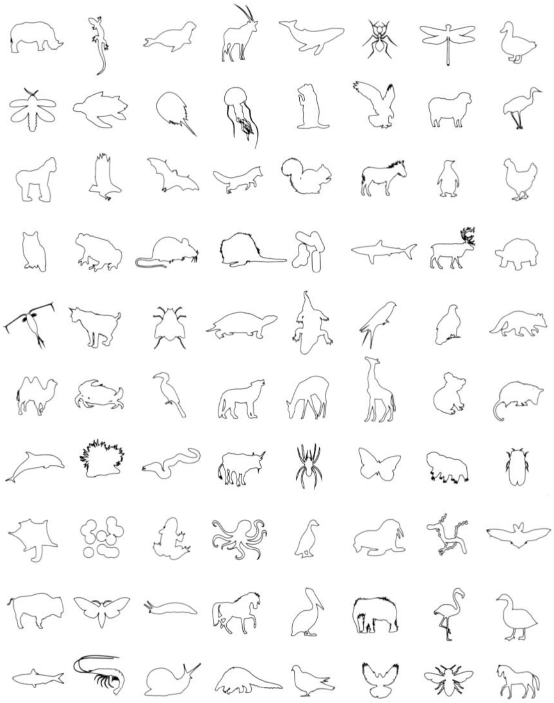

LA+ CREATURE
EDITORIAL

Throughout history landscape architecture has typically prioritized humans and plants over animals. It may be, however, that the animal, long neglected by the field, is becoming an increasingly important way into understanding and reenvisaging the landscapes of the Anthropocene. Animals provide key ecosystem services, they serve as mascots for larger environmental issues, and efforts to preserve them can galvanize communities. More than this, recent scholarship and advocacy points to the bigger idea that quite apart from what they can do or mean for us, animals have their own lives. And just as we value our own, theirs also warrant our respect and moral consideration.

Now, for the first time in the history of design a movement of actively cocreating with animals is emerging and it was this movement that the LA+ CREATURE design competition sought to consolidate. Judged by landscape architects Kate Orff, Andrew Grant, Chris Reed, and Farre Nixon, along with the former Dean of Environmental Design at University of California, Berkeley, Jennifer Wolch, and ecological philosopher Timothy Morton, the LA+ CREATURE competition attracted 258 entries from 31 countries.

Specifically, the competition asked "whether we can live with animals in new ways, whether we can transcend the dualism of decimation on the one hand and 'fortress conservation' on the other, and how we can use design to open our cities, our landscapes, and our minds to a more symbiotic existence with other creatures." Entrants were then required to do three things: choose a nonhuman creature (any species, any size, anywhere) and identify its needs (energy, shelter, procreation, movement, interaction, environment, etc.); design (or redesign) a place, structure, thing, system, and/or process that improves the creature's life; and contribute, through the design, to increasing human awareness of and empathy for the creature's existence. The jury chose five equal winning entries and awarded 10 honorable mentions.

In 2017, Marcus Owens and Jennifer Wolch scoured design websites and blogs for projects concerning animals to see if they could draw some general conclusions. Of 86 mainly hypothetical projects produced during the period 2000–2014, they found that 72 were for vertebrates (including 12 bats or birds), 12 were for arthropods (including seven bees), and two for other invertebrates. In addition to the fact that birds, bats, and bees seemed to be popular among designers, their conclusion was that most designs were more a form of "architectural practice as brand-building in the contemporary moment...rather than designing for animals per se. By comparison, of the 258 designs proposed in the LA+ CREATURE competition, 69 were for invertebrates (including 53 arthropods), 171 for vertebrates, and 18 for miscellaneous other creatures (including microbes and fungi). While there certainly were a considerable number of birds, bats, and bees among them (48, 12, and 12 respectively), submissions ranged across an impressively broad spectrum of creatures from large to small, wild to domestic, familiar to unknown, and friendly to deadly. And the designs were largely focused on the welfare of creatures, including interventions to address human exploitation of animals, to rethink the way in which we live and work with animals, and to restore habitats and food sources devastated through human action or inaction. Furthermore, many entrants sought to meet animals on their own terms and challenged the complicated problem of distanciation between us and them.

This issue of LA+ documents all the awarded entries, as well as a *Salon des Refuses* of entries that, for both conceptual and graphic reasons, caught the judges' eyes. To help make sense of this fascinating collection of work, each member of the jury responds to the same set of interview questions. And to close, we feature an essay by Lori Gruen, a leading scholar in critical animal studies, where she discusses the work and helps us understand it in its broader philosophical context.

LA+ sincerely thanks all those who participated.

Tatum L. Hands + Richard Weller
Issue Editors

LORI GRUEN

CREATURELY ENTANGLEMENTS

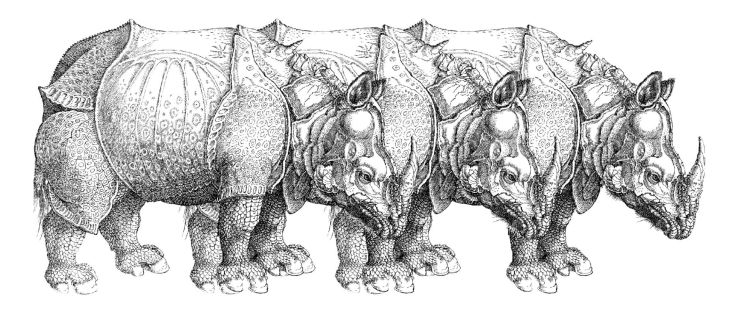

The more coherent one becomes within oneself as a creature, the more fully one enters into the communion of all creatures.[1]

Wendell Berry

Lori Gruen is the William Griffin Professor of Philosophy and coordinator of Animal Studies at Wesleyan University in Connecticut. She is the author and editor of 11 books, including *Entangled Empathy* (2015), *Critical Terms for Animal Studies* (2018), *Ethics and Animals* (2011), and *Ethics of Captivity* (2014). Gruen documented the history of the first 100 chimpanzees used in biomedical and behavioral research in the US and maintains the evolving website *The Last 1,000* [http://last1000chimps. com], which follows the journey to retirement of the last 1,000 chimpanzees to serve in this capacity in the US.

✛ ANIMAL STUDIES, ETHICS

Above: *The Rhinoceros* by Albrecht Dürer.

Recently, the *New York Times Magazine* published an in-depth story about the death of Sudan, the last male northern white rhinoceros on Earth.[2] Sudan died a few years before the story ran, on March 19, 2018, after living a long, transcontinental life. His death was movingly described in Sam Armstrong's stunning piece that explores a particularly elaborate, and in all likelihood, doomed, conservation effort to save this subspecies from extinction. Though Sudan was the last male, two females remain, his daughter Najin, and his grand-daughter Fatu. Neither have been able to reproduce, but there is a scientific hope, perhaps better described as sci-fi or fantasy, that their eggs may be used to eventually produce offspring. The Institute for Conservation Research at the San Diego Zoo has created a Frozen Zoo® that contains over 10,000 cells, eggs, sperm, and embryos from 1,000 species, including the northern white rhino.[3] They have 12 cell lines developed from Sudan's kind, and their goal is to develop stem cells to create sperm, and perhaps use Najin and Fatu's eggs, to create an embryo that will be implanted into a reproductively successful southern white rhinoceros in an attempt to re-establish a sustainable population. Armstrong describes this as "a reproductive hail Mary" as the odds are stacked against a successful birth, and even if baby northern white rhinos are born, the problems with keeping them alive in the wild are daunting. Without armed guards, even in protected territory, the remaining two females would surely be dead already. As Armstrong notes, "Some billionaire would no doubt pay a fortune to own the horns of the last two northern whites."[4]

Whether rich or poor, *Homo sapiens* have wreaked havoc on the planet and the other creatures who live on it. In May 2019, the United Nations reported that around one million animal and plant species are threatened with extinction.[5] In addition to the northern white rhino, the Javan, Sumatran, and western black rhinos are effectively extinct. Orangutans in Borneo and Sumatra are expected to be extinct in roughly a decade. Various tortoises, bats, and many different toads, frogs, lizards, and other amphibians have been classified as extinct. Insects are going extinct at alarming rates, although it is hard to determine actual numbers. The population of monarch butterflies has been consistently tracked and is now down 90% from 20 years ago; that is approximately 900 million butterflies gone.[6] Bumblebee and many spider populations have drastically declined. Polar bears, giant pandas, Cross River gorillas, and other megafauna are at great risk, as are hundreds of less charismatic creatures like eels, clams, and birds. Size, lifeways, and years on this Earth (it is estimated that rhinoceros have roamed the planet for 50 million years, a long run that is close to its end) don't stop the catastrophe unfolding around us.

No place is safe. We are heating the seas and leaving them strewn with plastic detritus degrading the ecosystems of the world's oceans. We've had a similar impact on land-based ecosystems. It is estimated, for instance, that a billion animals were killed by the fires that scorched Australian landscapes during the first few weeks of the hot season 2019–2020. These human-generated cataclysms haven't spared the animals who soar through the skies. Billions of birds have vanished in nearly all areas of North America since the 1970s. LA+ CREATURE could not be more timely and illuminating in the shadow of this anthropogenic mass extinction. The brief and designs help us to imagine different, more empathetic and symbiotic, ways of living with other creatures, ways that may sustain us all.

In one of the winning designs, Catherine Valverde, Youzi Xu, and Elizabeth Servito focus on the deleterious impact of human encroachment on the watershed that was home to the California tiger salamander. They propose repurposing golf courses to restore wetland habitats for the salamanders using three strategies, "vegetate, separate, and celebrate." The plan calls for restoring vegetation to support vernal pools, separating salamanders from humans to avoid damage from foot and car traffic, and celebrating the beauty of the shift from golf course greens to a Californian botanical garden. I'd like to broaden our thinking with these strategies, in the hope of revealing tensions and opportunities for reimagining our vexed relations with the more than human world.

While vegetating in the context of landscape design has a distinctive meaning, in a more colloquial and metaphorical sense, the term is often applied derogatorily to humans to liken them to plants. As young environmentalists like Greta Thunberg chastise policy makers for their inaction in the face of climate catastrophe, we might say that most humans are indeed vegetating as the planet burns. But that is unfair to plants that are sometimes more active than commonly thought. Interesting, although controversial, scientific research has suggested that humans may be "more plant-like than we would like to think, just as plants are more animal-like than we usually assume."[7] Our general passivity has allowed destructive human consumption and the extractive industries that support it to go largely unnoticed and unchecked, essentially condoning the status quo. This sort of inertia is just one side of vegetation, however. The other, of course, is growing and thriving in all sorts of conditions, hospitable or not. Perhaps we can reimagine vegetating as a process that quiets the mind so that new ideas can sprout – a helpful strategy in the face of the growing crises.

Many of the designs for LA+ CREATURE adopt the second strategy of separating humans from the animal "clients" in order to protect the creatures while at the same time highlighting their unique life worlds. Separation can provide animals space to attend to their social and material needs and desires without worrying about ever-present human encroachment. This opportunity is particularly important for social animals, allowing them to deepen relations with others of their kind, to develop specific cultures, to communicate, to play, and to create. Individual flourishing, in humans as well as other animals, crucially depends on a sustaining and sustainable space to be more than separate individuals and relish experiences with conspecifics and kin. Conscientiously separating them from us by creating protective, sometimes prosthetic, habitats provides new opportunities for them to thrive. It also provides humans with the opportunity to both rectify prior destruction and to see anew the ways other beings live, love, move, and ultimately die.

Yet separation is arguably the most powerful force that has led us to the planetary, as well as the political, crises we now face. Separation is a necessary part of the process of othering that grounds the oppression of those picked out as different. Racial and gender binaries are central categories of othering, as is the separation of humans from nonhumans. That humans are variously thought to be "at the top of the food chain" or "closer to God" or "outside of nature," and other animals (as well as *Homo sapiens* deemed not quite human) are considered less valuable, has served as a justification not just of exclusion, but instrumentalization, exploitation, and indifference.

Separation can also obscure the ways in which we are variously entangled. There is a common illusion that we can escape the relationships we are in, separate ourselves, whoever those selves are, from others. Of course, we can separate some animals from others for everyone's good, and we can separate ourselves in many instances from harmful and troubling others. But we are all, deeply, inseparably, entangled with others. We can't always, perhaps ever, fully transcend the relationships we are in but we can work to understand and improve them, in part, by improving our own self-conceptions. As Wendell Berry observes in the epigraph above, making one's self coherent and intelligible will allow us to more fully engage with others. Our relationships with human and animal others co-constitute who we are and how we configure our identities and agency, our thoughts and desires. We can't make coherent sense of living without others, and that includes other animals. We are entangled in complex relationships and we can't separate from all of them. Rather than imagining that separation is always a viable strategy we may do better to think about how to be more perceptive and more responsive in our entangled relationships.

That we are already in relations should ground our desires to more conscientiously reflect and engage with others. Since we exist in relation with other organisms, and our perceptions, attitudes, even our identities, are entangled with them and our actions make their experiences better or worse, which in turn affects our own experiences, we have good reasons for focusing our attention on these social/natural entanglements. That attention can lead us to want to improve on these relationships as we don't want to be in "bad" or "abusive" ones. Since we are already, inevitably in relationships, it makes sense to work to make them better, more meaningful, and more mutually satisfying. But recognizing that we are inevitably in relationships, replete with vulnerability and dependency, doesn't mean that we should accept those relationships as they are. Not all relationships are equally defensible. Relationships of exploitation or instrumentalization are precisely the sorts of relationships that we should work to imagine changing.

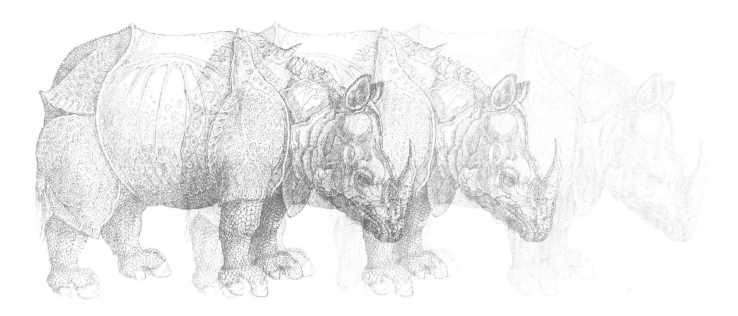

Importantly, we are not just in relationships as selves with others, but the self is comprised of what Karen Barad calls "intra-actions." Barad argues that the idea of "intra-action queers the familiar sense of causality (where one or more causal agents precede and produce an effect) and more generally unsettles the metaphysics of individualism (the belief that there are individually constituted agents or entities, as well as times and places)."[8] What this means is that there is not an individual that exists prior to and separate from the entangled intra-actions that constitute them. But, importantly, the individual that emerges from her entanglements is distinctly constituted by particular intra-actions. Understanding and reflecting on our entanglements is part of what it takes to constitute our selves.[9] There is no self or other prior to our intra-actions.

While everyone is entangled with others and to some extent with various forms and forces of life, there also are separate embodied beings who organize their perceptions and attitudes as a self, however porous, vulnerable, or shifting her boundaries may be. Most discussions of how to think about our relationships with other animals fail to attend to the particularity of individual animals. The category "creature" itself obscures important differences and relationships. Beavers, birds, and bats are animals, but we are in different relationships with each. Particular relationships with some birds, like owls, gives us virtually no context for understanding and empathizing with other birds, like pelicans, and the same holds true for bats. And within each group, there are individuals who have distinct personalities and likes and dislikes that get overlooked when we fail to separate them out.

We are in a continuous dance between othering and sameness, separation and entanglement. In response to othering, there is often a cry for inclusion, but these are awkward pleas as inclusion has tended to lean toward sameness rather than difference – "we too are human," "we too are valuable," "we too matter." Inclusion often is based on likenesses with those at the center; chimpanzees are more like human children than chinchilla or coral are. This process of "saming" then leaves those who are too different beyond our grasp. Importantly, those within the valued category themselves, who may also be different, will have their differences ignored or overlooked by saming forms of inclusion. When what we are focused on is similarities—how general types of intelligence or cognitive skills are shared, or some sensitivities and vulnerabilities are shared, or the same emotional responses are shared—distinctively valuable aspects of the lives of others become obscured. In failing to attend to separate ways of being, we ignore valuable aspects of different lives. There may be occasions when pointing out similarities has a strategic function, perhaps to call attention to those who have been denied recognition. But in doing that, the obfuscating impulses of saming and the too quick retreat to separation need to be regularly kept in check.

Dancing between recognition of our robust entanglements and appreciation of our distinctness is one way to celebrate the magnificence of the more than human world. But in this celebration, as in perhaps most celebrations, we inevitably encounter loss. Huong Dinh's honorable mention design presents a clever way of moving from loss to celebration, death to life, passivity to engagement. She proposes an alternative curriculum, the "Life of L" for young people who are ordinarily introduced to the northern leopard frog drenched in formaldehyde, taking students out of the biology lab and into the world to see frogs anew and alive, in a holistic, immersive encounter. It is a terrific celebration of the complexities of the failures and possibilities in our relationships with others. L is, as Dinh notes, no longer an abstraction, but "a protagonist in their own story with their unique worldview." Frogs, birds, beavers, octopus, walruses, spiders, cicada, crab, eels, and many other creatures make their own distinct meanings in the world, but though they may have individual worldviews, our world and theirs are inextricably entangled. Our encounters can be harsh and extractive, we can kill or sicken them, and they can pass along deadly pathogens to us. Alternatively, as Donna Haraway suggests, we can make kin with other creatures.[10] In so doing we will take on responsibilities that require that we not only learn about the worldviews of others, but empathetically work to try to understand what would make their lives better and bring about the conditions that make that possible. Imagine if we all had a brief encouraging us to redesign the world to improve all of our creaturely lives. That would really be something to celebrate.

1 Wendell Berry, *What are People For?* (Counterpoint, 2010), 11.

2 Sam Anderson, "The Last Two Northern White Rhinos on Earth," *The New York Times Magazine* (January 6, 2021) https://www. nytimes.com/2021/01/06/magazine/the-last-two-northern-white-rhinos-on-earth.html.

3 Institute for Conservation Research, "White Rhino," https://institute.sandiegozoo.org/ species/white-rhino (accessed January 30, 2021).

4 Anderson, "The Last Two Northern White Rhinos on Earth."

5 United Nations, "UN Report: Nature's Dangerous Decline 'Unprecedented'; Species Extinction Rates 'Accelerating," https:// www.un.org/sustainabledevelopment/ blog/2019/05/nature-decline-unprecedented-report/ (accessed January 30, 2021).

6 Brook Jarvis, "The Insect Apocalypse is Here," *The New York Times Magazine* (November 27, 2018) https://www. nytimes.com/2018/11/27/magazine/insect-apocalypse.html.

7 Josh Gabbatiss, "Plants can See, Hear, Smell – and Respond," *BBC Earth* (January 10, 2017) http://www.bbc.com/earth/story/20170109-plants-can-see-hear-and-smell-and-respond.

8 Karen Barad, *Meeting the Universe Half-way* (Duke, 2007); Karen Barad, "Intra-actions," *Mousse Magazine* 34 (2012).

9 For a fuller discussion of entanglement see Lori Gruen, *Entangled Empathy* (Lantern, 2014).

10 Donna Haraway, *Staying with the Trouble: Making Kin in the Chthulucene* (Duke, 2016).

The Jury

Nixeedorff morantolch

JURY Q+A

Andrew Grant is founder and director of Grant Associates, UK, and a visiting professor at the University of Sheffield. He is designer of the award-winning Gardens by the Bay and Supertree Grove in Singapore. In 2012 Grant was awarded the title of RSA Royal Designer for Industry in recognition of his pioneering global work in landscape architecture. He is currently collaborating on projects exploring the future of zoo experiences and endangered species conservation in Singapore and the UK.

Kate Orff is the founding principal of SCAPE and director of the Urban Design Program and Center for Resilient Cities and Landscapes at Columbia University's Graduate School of Architecture, Planning, and Preservation. She is known for leading complex, creative, and collaborative work processes that advance broad environmental and social prerogatives. In 2017 Orff was awarded the prestigious MacArthur Foundation Fellowship and in 2019 she received the Cooper Hewitt National Design Award in Landscape Architecture.

Chris Reed is founding director of Stoss Landscape Urbanism, as well as professor in practice of landscape architecture and co-director of the Master of Landscape Architecture in Urban Design Program at the Harvard Graduate School of Design. He is coauthor (with Nina-Marie Lister) of *Projective Ecologies* (2014). Reed received the 2012 Cooper Hewitt National Design Award in Landscape Architecture and was the 2017 Mercedes T. Bass Landscape Architect in Residence at the American Academy in Rome.

Jennifer Wolch is emeritus dean of the College of Environmental Design at the University of California, Berkeley and William W. Wurster Professor of City and Regional Planning. Wolch is author or editor of a number of books including *Animal Geographies: Place, Politics and Identity in the Nature-Culture Borderlands* (1998). Her work in this area includes studies of intersectionality and attitudes toward animals, urban design, and planning for multispecies cities, urban rewilding, and animals in contemporary design culture.

Farre Nixon is a landscape designer at Kounkuey Design Initiative in Los Angeles and a graduate of MIT and the University of Pennsylvania's Weitzman School of Design. With degrees in planning, architecture, and landscape architecture, Nixon is a strong advocate for transdisciplinary and collaborative practice and believes that the scope of work required to address the challenges of the Anthropocene presents an opportunity to enrich and transform design practice, expanding the paradigms within which architecture and landscape operate.

Timothy Morton is professor and Rita Shea Guffey Chair in English at Rice University, and author of *Being Ecological* (2018), *Dark Ecology* (2016), and *Hyperobjects* (2013), among other publications. Morton's 2017 book *Humankind: Solidarity with Nonhuman People* explores the separation between humans and nonhumans from an object-oriented ontological perspective, arguing that humans need to radically rethink the way in which they conceive of, and relate to, nonhuman animals and nature as a whole, and exploring the political implications of such a change.

+ The work in this competition is produced by an animal that has historically acclaimed its own exceptionalism – unlike other animals we have words, numbers, foresight, free will, society, cities, and, above all, gods...or so many believe. Taking the competition results as a whole, what do you think it tells us about human exceptionalism at this moment in time?

Andrew Grant: The competition highlights that we don't really know how best to repair our ecological self-harm and we are just at the beginning of a journey to rediscover our innate "animalness." As the sculptor Antony Gormley said: "We are all bloody animals...its really weird that with all our technology, with all our instruments, with all our intelligence, still we are really basic." I think in all cases the solutions implied we, as humans, know best. We think we know what other species want, we think we know how to repair their world. I don't think there was a proposition that defined a human no-go zone to allow the species to adapt in its own way free from human influence. Many were actually the opposite, exploring how to optimize the benefit of a species for our entertainment or for food or medicine.

Kate Orff: There is a gradient of consciousness with all living things–including plants and animals–communicating their needs with the larger biosphere. However, there is a clear break within this gradient in terms of power and control – humans have developed guns, weapons of mass destruction, and committed ecocide on a broad scale as we make more space for ourselves. Humans have the power to erase, fragment, mourn, and document the loss of other species but have not (yet) embraced the power to work holistically and knit the fabric of landscape back together to support biodiversity.

Chris Reed: *In Steps Toward an Ecology of Mind* (1972), Gregory Bateson offers the following revelatory and cautionary observation: "we are not outside the ecology for which we plan – we are always and inevitably a part of it. Herein lies the charm and terror of ecology." This passage, like "Earthrise," the photograph of the Earth taken in 1968 by Apollo 8 astronaut William Anders, reminds us of how inextricably entwined we are, as humans, with the world around us; and that, while we are *part of it*, as Bateson points out, the world still exists autonomously – irrespective of our existence as a single species. The LA+ CREATURE competition entries remind me very much of both our exceptional and unexceptional positions within this world, within this cosmos. The multitude of organisms represented reveals a world of unexplored perspectives and lenses on the design project and on the larger social project of the environment. These include the complex ecologies that may allow such creatures to persist and thrive; the interdependent habitats that can be created to allow for interactions between and among creatures and humans; and the weaving of narratives around Animalia that have marked human society for generations – narratives that again speak to the inherent interrelatedness of things. These perspectives offer two complementary imperatives. First, responding as designers to the climate crisis– and, more broadly, to the world around us–must entail attention to a fuller array of creatures and conditions than those that are simply human-focused, and human-settlement-focused. Yet this environmental awareness is not enough, at least within the design disciplines. Second, then, these acknowledgments of human–creature and creature–Earth codependencies offer new, rich lenses through which we may and must design, through which we may imagine future conditions and future worlds – new opportunities for design thinking and advancement that moves beyond the human gaze alone.

Jennifer Wolch: The competition entries reveal an awareness of animals as species that are not only essential parts of global and local ecosystems, but are also individual subjects-of-a-life that possess their own remarkable capabilities and ways of living in the world. Some were anthropocentric in orientation, focusing on how interventions supporting an animal could benefit people. But most revealed ways of thinking about–and designing for/with–the nonhuman world that reject human exceptionalism and the radical anthropocentrism from which it springs, on the basis of scientific evidence and the deep harm this idea has inflicted on individual animals, the web of life, and the entire planet.

1 Jennifer Wolch & Marcus Owens, *"Animals in Contemporary Architecture and Design," Humanimalia: A Journal of Human/Animal Interface Studies* 8, no. 2 (2017) 1–26.

Previous: Image by Aaron Stone.

Farre Nixon: A few days ago, I read an article about a group of researchers who discovered that kangaroos–thought to be wild animals–were intentionally communicating with them. After attempting and failing tests to open containers of food, the frustrated kangaroos would look up and gaze at the researcher. Some kangaroos would go so far as to nudge or scratch the human as a plea for help to open the containers. These findings are significant because they challenge our prevailing assumption that domesticated animals are the only creatures that purposely communicate with humans in ways we can interpret. Upon reading this article, my first thought was, "How absurd." It's not the kangaroos or the experiment I found absurd. It's the idea that we've assumed (for who knows how long) that wild animals would never–could never–try to communicate with us. Knowing the ways in which humans have dramatically shaped and altered this planet and the habitats of most, if not all, animals, it is absolutely preposterous to think that these creatures have not previously attempted interspecies communication to warn, chide, petition, thwart, or even curse us. Whether motivated by science, religion, or empathy, if more people took the time to actually observe other animals – animal livelihoods, habits, and struggles – we'd be amazed at what we would learn. The LA+ CREATURE competition sets the stage for this kind of observation. The brief itself demands the human designer step outside of herself and imagine what services, material goods, or other interventions a nonhuman client might request of a human. With the skills, abilities, and power we humans have claimed and currently wield, what might we do under the service of a nonhuman?

Timothy Morton: The value of this competition was that it inspired people to work fast on something that requires urgent, urgent, work. I don't know how obvious it is to enough people that we are undergoing a mass extinction event, caused primarily by human destruction of the biosphere. It's terrifying. I can hardly think about it. I commend everyone who entered something for this competition, because it's so urgent and the issue is so painful and frightening. We have to be able to hold two thoughts in our head at the same time. Ready? Number one, we are no better than and no different from other lifeforms. Number two, we did this. People in my line of work get confused about the word Anthropocene. They think it's a compliment, whereas it is in fact the greatest insult ever, like finding your house has been replaced by a pile of all the shit you excreted throughout your life.

+ In 2017 researchers scoured design websites and blogs for projects concerning animals to see if they could draw some general conclusions. Of 86 mainly hypothetical projects produced during the period 2000–2014, they found that pets received a lot of design attention but our closest evolutionary relatives, the great apes, did not. Neither did animals we use for food or milk. They also concluded that most works were a form of "architectural practice as brand-building in the contemporary moment... rather than designing for animals per se."[1] Thinking about the range of proposals presented by entrants in LA+ CREATURE, what would your conclusions be?

Andrew Grant: I think the proposals submitted fell into several distinct groups. First, those that focused on land management changes to facilitate better opportunities for the selected species. Essentially how you would imagine an ecologically minded landscape architect would respond. Secondly, those that explored sci-fi storytelling as a way to radically reimagine our relationship with individual species and allowing the story to embrace the planetary and global context. Thirdly, those that created highly artificial technological habitat/structures to support the species, often in strange and patently non-organic forms. Fourthly, those that gave credence to the rights of other species through the creation of a legal and conservation framework for species-specific urban habitat management. Fifthly, those that sought a way to deliver greater empathy for individual species. And finally, those that played with their food.

Kate Orff: I was fascinated by how, as a whole, all of the entries point out gaps in scales of impact of designed landscapes. We can make a bird house, or a small park with food and forage for neo-tropical migrants, but if the entire Mississippi delta wetland system has collapsed, we are still headed for incredible loss of avian species and the aesthetic and moral horror that entails.

Chris Reed: The range of creatures featured here is a reminder of the incredible richness and diversity of global fauna, including animals that aren't traditionally considered "lovable" by widespread audiences or worthy of design attention: spiders, desert rain frogs, bats, vultures, soldier flies, eels, paper silverfish – a Noah's ark of all things icky and ugly. Many of these creatures are indifferent toward humans, except to the extent that we are negatively impacting their habitats and ways of life. Finding value in things that exist beyond the typical scope of human attention and care is perhaps one of the most important contributions of this competition.

Jennifer Wolch: I was heartened to see so many entries *not* designed to build a brand or attract online attention. These entries generally paid serious attention to the animal's natural history, ecology, and behavior, and tried to "think like the animal" in designing interventions on their behalf. Interestingly, there were almost no designs for companion animals. That said there was still no focus on great apes or the billions of animals raised, slaughtered, and eaten by humans each year. For very different reasons, such animals are uncomfortably close to us. The apes are our nearest cousins yet end up as bush meat, imprisoned in biomedical research labs, or sold into captivity by illegal animal smugglers. The sheer magnitude and horrendous cruelty of animal slaughter for food make most people look away, feel guilty or defensive about their dietary habits, and/or believe themselves helpless to effect change. I encourage environmental designers to engage with great apes or so-called "food" animals as clients, and develop new design interventions that address the severe injustices inflicted on these animals.

Farre Nixon: Domesticated creatures are under our care and control; therefore, it is no surprise they receive the bulk of the little attention designers put toward animal architecture. In the case of CREATURE, however, that has been the contrary. The range of nonhuman clients exhibited throughout the competition was both surprising and refreshing. From elephants to silverfish, the competition engaged clients big and small. There were a lot of birds, though!

Timothy Morton: This [research finding] is quite odd. Of course we design for "animals we use for food and milk." It's called feed lots. We do design for them! We just design terrible, violent death camps, is all. Animals used for food and milk... that's a euphemism and a half. And it's not just that it's diabolical for sentient beings. Agriculture is responsible for a huge amount of global heating. The good news is that eating a lot less or no meat is the one thing you can do as an individual to fight against global heating. It's awful to feel so powerless. Connect to larger groups and collectives, of any size and scale – they can overlap and don't need to cancel each other out. And go as completely vegan as you possibly can. There is no point in designing anything more in the line of "using animals for food and milk." It would be great if architects could start a movement for real homes for these lifeforms, in solidarity with them. I would like to see that.

+ What did you find most compelling and most disappointing about the proposals?

Andrew Grant: On one, perhaps superficial, level I was struck by how beautiful many of the drawings and graphics were and wondered if this was directly inspired by the species in question or whether all the authors were just genius communicators. The graphic array of different colors, styles, and complexity mirrored the diversity of species on show and I think the collective pictorial impression of all of these ideas is perhaps more compelling than any single entry. It reflects the urgency and energy we need to apply to fix biodiversity loss. I was disappointed that many of the entries tried to create abstracted habitats that reflected a human aesthetic and wondered if any had imagined what they designed through the eyes and skills of their selected individual species. We know many animals, birds, and insects create their own world through design so how could we enhance those skills and be agents of species not masters of species? I was also disappointed that very few of the entries tried to imagine the interrelationships and interconnectedness with other species and how their ideas would enhance or facilitate the creation of new ecologies.

Kate Orff: I found the proposals that demanded a human response or change in personal behavior (slowing down, reducing consumption, etc.) compelling. Projects that just proposed an artificial stand-in for a physical missing ecosystem component (like an artificial tree) were, to me, on the disappointing side.

Chris Reed: I was most compelled by sheer inventiveness of idea or approach where the design expression was embedded in the creature or habitat agenda, for example, in the Chinese pangolin proposal [Yi Lu + Ruomin Jiang – Salon des Refusés]; where the very needs of a creature like the horseshoe crab [Niko Dellic + Ambika Pharma – Winner] could implicate the recycling of civilization's waste and simultaneously make for new and enigmatic human experiences; or where intelligent shifts in policy or operations might lead to a palpable, experiential result – even when the connections were not immediately obvious, for example, in the case of the "Cicada Code" entry [Conor O'Shea – Honorable Mention]. I was least compelled by proposals that either positioned the human as a mere spectator in a larger habitat (these felt too much like a voyeuristic zoo experience separating us from them), or that tended more toward restoration ecology than design. This is not to say that design expression needs to dominate, but these were proposals in which the connections to humans as a force in the making of these places were less visible or nonexistent. Perhaps that's okay if we understand that creatures can exist without humans and human intervention. But given that all proposals were in some way or another informed by a change in policy and/or regulation and/or physical intervention, shouldn't we allow space for the expression of that human hand – even if only to serve a non-human agenda?

Jennifer Wolch: For me, the most compelling proposals were those that displayed deep knowledge and understanding of the animal "clients" based on the scientific literature; thought carefully about how to codify their solution into law or weave it into everyday practice; considered how to generalize their site-specific ideas into broader geographies; and stayed focused on the animal's needs versus those of people. The proposals that I found disappointing fell into two categories. One category included anthropocentric designs that involved animals but used them to serve humans in some fashion (although some of these were inventive and beautifully visualized). The other category included projects that relied on radical new technologies. Often these technologies were unconvincing because they were untested, were not buildable, involved massive insertions in the environment that would create more problems than they solved, or were too intrusive to gain public acceptance.

Farre Nixon: The majority of respondents genuinely attempted to address a unique and complex issue their animal client faced. Reading through the supporting statements was an education in and of itself; I learned an immense amount about current-day problems specific to a wide variety of nonhuman species. These problems often arose from human-animal habitat adjacencies many of us are unaware of. Shortlisted entrants masterfully articulated these problems and their proposed, innovative solutions through a limited number of visualizations, which I found extremely impressive. After reviewing the first 10 entries, however, I quickly discovered a trend that became somewhat disappointing. The design approach many entrants took became formulaic, often following the same series of steps. The formula was along these lines: here's my animal client >> here are some animal facts about my client >> here is a human-caused problem that afflicts my client >> here is a human-mediated object to fix my client's problem >> and, finally, here is an image of my client happily interacting with this object that is now permanently embedded into their environment. In general, there was a lack of acknowledgment of the agency that nonhumans inherently possess. This is a difficult, radical task to do, and few entrants did it well. I was much more interested in the entries that took this to heart, exploring new approaches and other possibilities.

Timothy Morton: The fact that they exist at all was compelling. I am also very touched to see designers working on things, because in whatever way, they try to make ideas and projects into sensual forms. The fact that there were so many proposals was wonderful. The way people visualized their projects was breathtaking for me, as someone who uses sentences and not software. The capacity to visualize a radically different future in the most holistic sense...I wanted some more of that. Crazy, beautiful utopian imaginings at Earth magnitude. Here's how to help one species: create global collective movements that have all lifeforms in mind. Architecture is a form of movement isn't it? Black Lives Matter and #MeToo arrived just in time. Black Lives Matter may be the largest movement the USA has ever seen, and it's truly international, because slavery is international. There's plenty of architecture for global corporations and transnational religions. Someone might have proposed something truly huge and "impossible." We need to think and feel at that scale and work at loads of other scales, at the same time. It's the only way this is going to work, by which I mean, this is the only way we have a chance of not destroying the biosphere beyond all recognition.

+ If design in relation to animals is ever to be more than a reiteration of the zoological (anthropocentric) gaze, then it presents us with the challenge of engaging with beings whose consciousness is in fact almost completely unavailable to us. Into this gap we place the catch-all and cure-all word "empathy." Can you identify moments in any of the entries where you felt the zoological gaze was being genuinely unsettled and empathy was being navigated in new or profound ways?

Andrew Grant: I thought quite a few entries tackled this in a really interesting way. I had to really think about the roadkill entry [Jacky Bowring – Salon des Refusés], which explored the unimagined consequences of our way of living and the need to rekindle empathy for dead animals killed by human action. There was also a fantastic idea about reframing the life of the northern leopard frog from being perceived only as a dead fixture in school kids' biology labs to one where the whole life cycle and live habitat of the frog is the focus [Huong Dinh – Honorable Mention]. Giving rights to species also seemed an interesting way to express empathy: for example, the proposal that outlined a compelling idea for using city ordnance rules to protect the 17-year life cycle of the cicada [Conor O'Shea – Honorable Mention]. Another entry brought focus to the water bear (tardigrade) and used storytelling to shift our understanding and empathy for this extraordinary creature [Goh Yu Han, Wong Mee Na + Yazid Ninsalam – Salon des Refusés].

Kate Orff: I found the story about horseshoe crabs and bloodletting wild and unsettling. We have depended on these animals and their miraculous blood for a range of critical medical tests. I wrote about the horseshoe crab in *Toward an Urban Ecology* (2016) and the demise of intertidal landscapes and shallow shoreline gradients – but this takes interdependence to a whole new level! Our blood and fluids are shared – we just don't see it that way. Moments like this competition, which shine light on our true physical and mental interdependence with nonhuman beings, are fantastic.

Chris Reed: In this sense, I was particularly struck by the proposal for the orb-weaver spider [Aitor Frías-Sánchez, Joaquín Perailes-Santiago + Aashti Miller – Honorable Mention], which employed advanced AI technology–and design–in pursuit of a rehabilitation agenda for spiders whose most characteristic and life-sustaining attribute (web making) has been damaged by human-caused radiation intensities in the Chernobyl Exclusion Zone. The proposal embedded a strategy for both deploying spider colonies and aiding in the making of webs, filling a gap caused by the species' exposure to radiation levels, and resulting in a collection of enigmatic pods that would be deployed and redeployed throughout the landscape. Most compelling here–and most empathetic, perhaps–was the dual rehabilitation agendas inherent in the project: first a strategy to help the spiders in creating their webs, and second by amplifying the spiders' plight through the very evident creation of the cyborg nests. For me, design here was employed with the dual purpose of advancing spider health and of instigating connection and catharsis in humans; it was also design as armature, as catalyst, with an authorship shaped and shared by the creatures for whom the proposal is imagined.

Jennifer Wolch: Three categories of entries went beyond expressions of "empathy." These are projects that used ethological/ecological/geophysical information about animal behavior to ground their design intervention ideas; others that creatively used anthropomorphism to help them "think" like the animal for whom they were designing; and projects that involved their animal clients in mutual learning experiments to develop or refine their designs.

Farre Nixon: When reviewing the competition entries, I immediately gravitated toward the proposals that offered no opportunities for the anthropocentric, zoological gaze. The blind, a device used to prevent animal detection of the human presence, became a design trend seen throughout many of the entries. I found this trend ironic, since it is exactly the uninvited, human presence that often exacerbates many of the issues that animals face. A good example of this irony occurred during the early months of the COVID-19 pandemic. It involves panda sex. A giant panda wildlife reserve in Hong Kong excitedly announced to the world that after 13 years of cohabitation, two of their pandas, Le Le and Ying Ying, finally successfully mated. It only took a global pandemic to shut out nosy human visitors from the center for the two pandas to get the privacy they deserved. Who can blame them?

One design that successfully and poetically circumvents this issue is the burial platform proposal [by Yushen Jia + Thomas Wang – Salon des Refusés]. Situated atop the Tibetan mountain peaks far away from the voyeuristic eyes of dark tourists, the proposed burial platforms offer up bodies of recently deceased humans to the Himalayan vulture. Although seemingly morbid by Western standards, the sky burial is a sacred, traditional rite that has been practiced by adherents of Tibetan Buddhism for thousands of years. Bodies are delivered by drone to the platform, where the only living things there render them to pieces. The only way a human can participate is if they're dead.

Timothy Morton: Architects, stop doing philosophy and listen to us. This question is like being clonked with a huge piece of rebar. It doesn't make sense. Is our own consciousness "available" to us? Prove it, now. You have 30 seconds. What is it, even? What does available mean? You can't just use words like stuff you order from that gigantic catalog. That's what got us into this mess. The zoological gaze is the least of our troubles, assuming for a moment that I understand what that means. I think it means "not the violence to moocows gaze." That's a gaze and a half.

+ Whereas the psychological and physical drama of human-animal interactions takes place at the site scale, the sixth extinction is taking place at a planetary scale. Did you find any of the work relevant in terms of how it might bridge this scale?

Andrew Grant: Several submissions attempted to address the scale of mass habitat loss by picking on habitats under threat such as ice caps, forests, and oceans. Others picked migration routes that cross multiple landscapes. I thought the entry about Pacific walruses [Zhou Wang – Honorable Mention] did begin to explore the enormous global challenge of adaptation for this species when accepting their original habitat will never ever be the same again due to the loss of ice sheets. However, by focusing on single species the global challenge will never really be tackled. Perhaps the next competition should upscale the ambition and explore ideas for whole systems and relationships of species and global management. LA+ ECOSYSTEM has a ring to it.

Kate Orff: I think literally any species can be a proxy for landscape-scale thinking, and when you start to combine and overlay these and make a competition that is global in scope you can start to see how the habitat mosaic that has sustained animals and people could be knitted back together. So, in their aggregate, yes, the work showed glimpses of a chance to take on the sixth extinction in all of its gravity.

Chris Reed: None of these proposals single-handedly solve the planetary challenges we currently face, and will face for some time to come – this is an impossible endeavor. Rather, as a group the proposals speak to the need for collective actions and collective solutions that have differential impacts at multiple scales and touch individual cultures in different ways. Many of the proposals were explicitly replicable at very small scales and within already built environments. Others spoke to the need for large-scale intervention but could be imagined as demonstrative of a strategy that could be replicated and tuned to different environments, climates, and creature needs. Imagine if all golf courses, for example, throughout a large country, across an entire continent, or around the world were altered to accommodate the habitat needs of a critical keystone species – the cumulative effects would indeed be planetary. Equally important, though—and very much to the point of this thought exercise—is the idea that such proposals and interventions can change cultural attitudes toward the creatures with whom we share the planet. The recognition of the importance of nonhuman lenses in the making and remaking of our lived environments are themselves impactful *social* acts that can have positive *environmental* effects for generations to come.

Jennifer Wolch: Several projects tackled extinction and threats to global biodiversity. For example, one entry focused on the plight of one walrus subspecies facing extinction due to loss of sea ice [Zhou Wang – Honorable Mention]. The intervention proposed a novel transport system that could save these walruses by towing them to a geographically separate subpopulation that enjoys ample sea ice habitat. Another considered the increased prevalence and destructiveness of forest wildfires driven by climate change, designing forest structures to help birds survive and thrive after such conflagrations burn through their tree habitat [Arthur Lam – Winner]. But it is important to note that design entries tackling localized or site-specific scales can be important in the struggle against extinction too. Such interventions may stave off local extirpation, deal with novel emergent ecosystems driven by climate change, or incorporate protections for species into local land-use codes. If implemented, such projects can have aggregative effects, inspire other places to adopt similar strategies, and show the range of design, policy, and planning tools that together can make a cumulative difference for a wide variety of animals.

Farre Nixon: While several of the proposals dealt with the issue of migration as it pertained to their particular animal client, almost all were situated squarely within the scale of the site. There were many references to the global nature of the extinction crisis, which was to be expected. What I didn't expect and was pleasantly surprised to see were entries dealing with the microbial scale. The microbiome has largely been ignored amongst the design world, likely because to understand it one must call upon a domain of knowledge outside of design – that of science. However, as a few entrants exhibited in their proposals, the marriage of science and design presents another lens through which to view our world. One entry demonstrated this in an expansive and eccentric proposal for a tardigrade telescope [Goh Yu Han, Wong Mee Na + Yazid Ninsalam – Salon des Refusés]. It's these kinds of projects that keep me optimistic about the avenues and opportunities the microbial realm presents for the designer-biologist in the future. Perhaps there are answers to our planetary-scale problems under the microscope.

Timothy Morton: The drama is taking place at all scales. Are you breathing oxygen right now? Good. You can read this sentence: bacterial poop is distributed pretty evenly across Earth after three-plus billion years of bacteria pooping, and that's why you can read this sentence. And is the extinction taking place at planet scale? A little rodent is dying in a bush. She is the last of her kind. Is that planet scale? As I said earlier, there wasn't nearly enough of imagining things at planet scale. One way to encourage more would be to stop thinking in binaries of psychological and physical (which is itself a toxic binary) versus planetary.

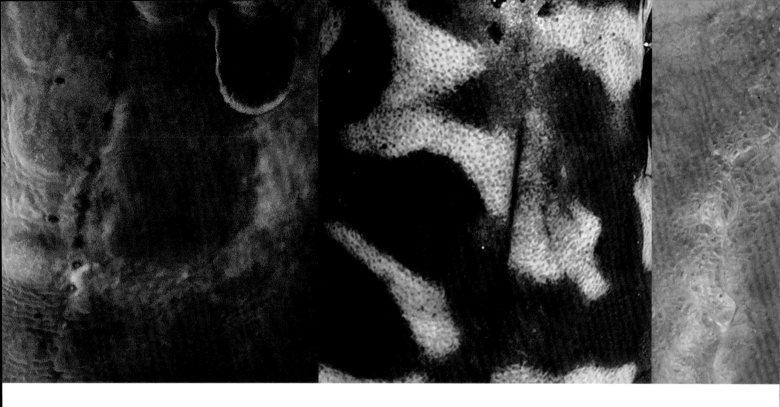

WINNING

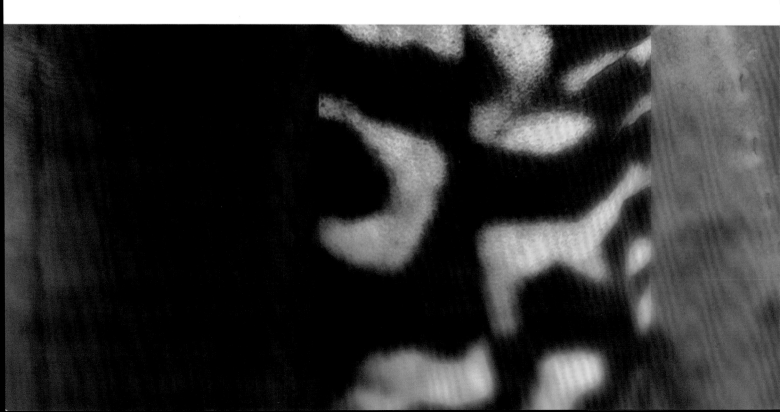

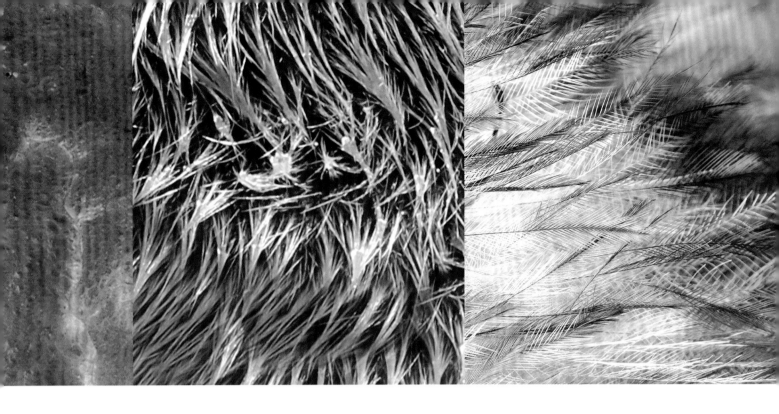

ENTRIES

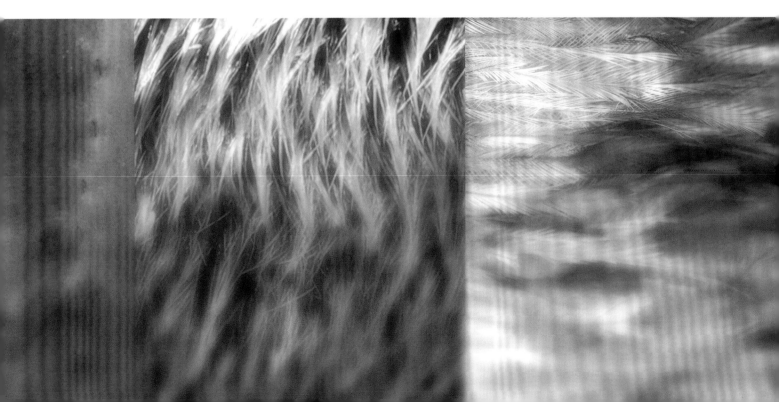

NIKO DELLIC
AMBIKA PHARMA

MANGROVE HORSESHOE CRAB

Carcinoscorpius rotundicauda

The blood of more than 500,000 horseshoe crabs is extracted every year to supply the biomedical field with lifesaving chemicals. Their blood cells are used as a detection system for harmful bacteria that could show up in vaccines and medical tools. With the anticipated development of five billion COVID-19 vaccines, blood harvesting will likely increase considerably. While synthetic alternatives have been developed and are awaiting approval from governing bodies, a replacement isn't necessarily beneficial for the crabs: they have been better protected in recent years as a resource for the biomedical field than in the previous century when their population was rapidly dwindling. The proposed strategy exists at the intersection of exploitation and conservation, proposing a regulatory law to guarantee the continued blood harvesting of horseshoe crabs, reserving synthetic alternatives for pandemics and abnormal demand.

The proposal is sited off Sagar Island, India, where climate change, coastal urban-ization, and fisheries have resulted in considerable habitat loss for the vulnerable Mangrove Horseshoe Crab. The design strives to reduce the mortality rate and increase the reproduction rate of the bled horseshoe crabs by creating synthetic mangroves on old shipping barges. These would act as harvesting and rehabilitation centers for what has been identified as a crucial two-week period where the bled horseshoe crabs are disoriented, weak, and have trouble spawning. The design of the synthetic mangroves includes shallow beach pools and lanterns with a blue hue (Purkinje effect) to simulate the light of a full moon, both of which are breeding stimulants for the horseshoe crab. From there, the crabs partake in a breeding process that is nothing short of an orgy.

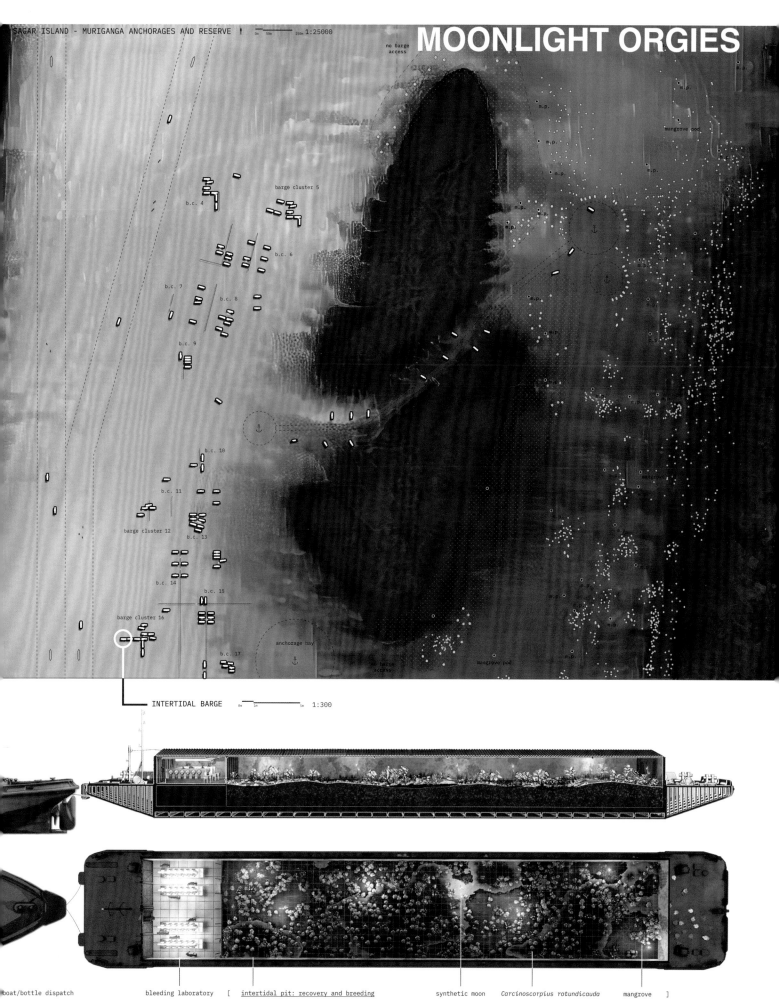

SAGAR ISLAND - MURIGANGA ANCHORAGES AND RESERVE   0m 50m   250m 1:25000

MOONLIGHT ORGIES

no barge
access

barge cluster 5

b.c. 4

b.c. 6

b.c. 7

b.c. 8

b.c. 9

b.c. 10

b.c. 11

barge cluster 12

b.c. 13

b.c. 14

b.c. 15

barge cluster 16

b.c. 17

anchorage bay

mangrove pod

INTERTIDAL BARGE   0m   1m   5m   1:300

boat/bottle dispatch   bleeding laboratory   [[intertidal pit: recovery and breeding   synthetic moon   *Carcinoscorpius rotundicauda*   mangrove   ]

ENVIRONMENTAL AMENDMENT 162/201

This Environmental Amendment is entered into by and between *Sagar Biomedical Corporation* (hereafter referred to as "Offeror") and *Wildlife Trust of India* (hereafter referred to as "Offeree").

RECITALS

A.   Offeror desires an ongoing 50% of matured Mangrove Horseshoe Crab or *Carcinoscorpius rotundicauda* for Tachypleus Amebocyte Lysate (TAL) extraction contingent on health of the threshold population at high priority zones (outlined in figure 1), on review by Wildlife Trust of India per the proposal and associated emails, and attachments exchanged on March 31, 2020 to October 10, 2020.

B.   Offeree desires habitat restoration of primary habitat zones along West Coast Bengal (Sagar Island, Bhitarkanika, with a minimum 8% of the target 150 kilometers of coastal edge enhancement), recovery facilities post-extraction of TAL, and relocation to spawning sites in primary habitat zones, per the proposal and associated emails, and attachments exchanged on March 31, 2020 to October 10, 2020.

NOW, THEREFORE:

1. Both parties agree that at minimum a threshold population must be maintained at high priority zones. Reciprocal services rendered by each party including protection from illegal trade, poaching and religious use will be as agreed to in proposals shared in and attached to emails exchanged on August 7, 2020, September 19, 2020 and October 10, 2020 between Offeror and Offeree.

2. Offeror acknowledges and agrees that Offeree's scope of representation is limited to the recitals contained in paragraph "A" of this Amendment and shall not include, without additional written agreement, any decrease in the scale of LAL production and baseline scale of inventory. And shall also not include or incur any non-service related risks associated with paragraph "A" of this Amendement.

3. Offeree acknowledges and agrees that Offeror's scope of representation is limited to the recitals contained in paragraph "B" of this Amendment and shall not include any non-service related fees or risks associated with paragraph "B" of this Amendment.

4. Both parties agree that they will complete their respective services in the time period referenceed in email and associated attachments. Both parties agree to the objectives that prevent, minimize. and within the limits of agreed upon services, elimates risks to *Carcinoscorpius rotundicauda* habitat and resources with specific attention to increasing spawning rates in high priority zones and maintaining egg survival rates in captivity above 85%.

5. Both parties agree that all non-service production necessary in the event of an increase of demand in vaccines or pandemic scenario, synthetic production of LAL will buffer agreed upon services as set by

YOUZI XU
ELIZABETH SERVITO
CATHERINE VALVERDE

CALIFORNIA TIGER SALAMANDER
Ambystoma californiense

As the air cools, little critters hiding in abandoned ground-squirrel tunnels emerge into the night. One wiggles out displaying an array of yellow spots. After months of rain, it's time for this California tiger salamander to migrate to her breeding ground. In the past, this six-inch, thick-bodied amphibian could travel to one of many vernal pools in the Ballona Creek Watershed. Today, her options are slim. The 130 m2 Ballona Creek watershed, once home to over 14,000 acres of salamander-friendly wetlands, is now home to 1.2 million people, with only 4% of the original wetland remaining. Watershed loss and mass extermination of native ground squirrels and gophers–whose burrows provide terrestrial homes to the California tiger salamander–have led to the collapse of the salamander population. But there is hope: golf courses could be affordable sites to restore wetlands.

We seek to redesign the Los Angeles Country Club to restore salamander habitats on golf courses through three strategies: vegetate, separate, and celebrate. To vegetate is to restore a diverse array of Californian plant comm-unities that withstand seasonal droughts and support vernal pools. Vegetation will be deployed depending on slope, aspect, and proximity to existing trees and development. To separate is to create a system of human paths and tunnels to protect animal habitats from foot traffic. Humans and animals can safely cross the 80-foot-wide Wilshire Boulevard using separate underpasses. The animal tunnel will have embedded sensors that transmit information on animal migration onto the surfaces of the human tunnel to increase awareness of the salamander population among human visitors. Finally, to celebrate a new Californian aesthetic, components of the European golf course will be replaced with a Californian botanical garden. As water from the wet season evaporates in spring rings of flowers encircle vernal pools, enhancing awareness of wetness gradients throughout the park topography.

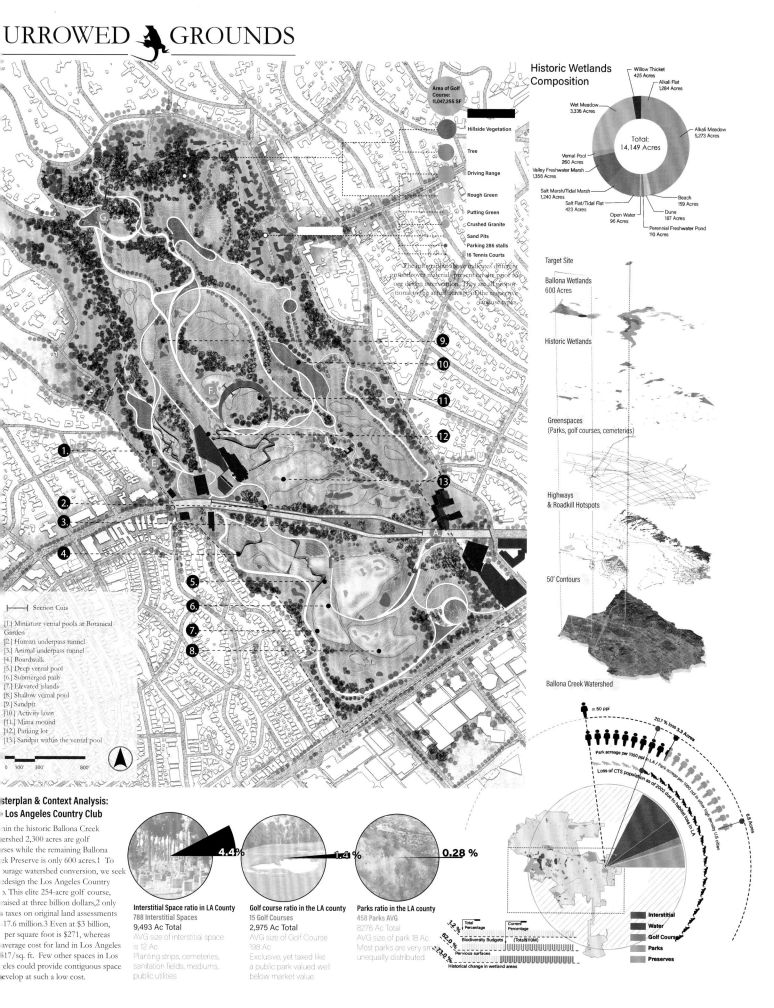

URROWED GROUNDS

Area of Golf Course: 11,047,255 SF

Legend:
- Hillside Vegetation
- Tree
- Driving Range
- Rough Green
- Putting Green
- Crushed Granite
- Sand Pits
- Parking 286 stalls
- 16 Tennis Courts

The infographic above indicates different groundcover materials present on site prior to our design intervention. They are all proportional to the actual acreage of the respective land-use types.

Historic Wetlands Composition

- Willow Thicket 425 Acres
- Alkali Flat 1,284 Acres
- Wet Meadow 3,336 Acres
- Alkali Meadow 5,273 Acres
- Vernal Pool 260 Acres
- Valley Freshwater Marsh 1,356 Acres
- Salt Marsh/Tidal Marsh 1,240 Acres
- Salt Flat/Tidal Flat 423 Acres
- Open Water 96 Acres
- Beach 159 Acres
- Dune 187 Acres
- Perennial Freshwater Pond 110 Acres

Total: 14,149 Acres

Target Site:
- Ballona Wetlands 600 Acres
- Historic Wetlands
- Greenspaces (Parks, golf courses, cemeteries)
- Highways & Roadkill Hotspots
- 50' Contours
- Ballona Creek Watershed

Section Cuts
[1.] Miniature vernal pools at Botanical Garden
[2.] Human underpass tunnel
[3.] Animal underpass tunnel
[4.] Boardwalk
[5.] Deep vernal pool
[6.] Submerged path
[7.] Elevated islands
[8.] Shallow vernal pool
[9.] Sandpit
[10.] Activity lawn
[11.] Mima mound
[12.] Parking lot
[13.] Sandpit within the vernal pool

0   100'   300'   800'

sterplan & Context Analysis: Los Angeles Country Club

hin the historic Ballona Creek ershed 2,300 acres are golf rses while the remaining Ballona ek Preserve is only 600 acres.1 To burage watershed conversion, we seek edesign the Los Angeles Country b. This elite 254-acre golf course, raised at three billion dollars,2 only taxes on original land assessments 17.6 million.3 Even at $3 billion, per square foot is $271, whereas average cost for land in Los Angeles 17/sq. ft. Few other spaces in Los eles could provide contiguous space evelop at such a low cost.

4.4% — Interstitial Space ratio in LA County
788 Interstitial Spaces
9,493 Ac Total
AVG size of interstitial space is 12 Ac
Planting strips, cemeteries, sanitation fields, mediums, public utilities

1.4% — Golf course ratio in the LA county
15 Golf Courses
2,975 Ac Total
AVG size of Golf Course 198 Ac
Exclusive, yet taxed like a public park valued well below market value

0.28% — Parks ratio in the LA county
458 Parks AVG
8276 Ac Total
AVG size of park 18 Ac
Most parks are very small unequally distributed.

= 50 ppl
20.7% loss 3.3 Acres
Park acreage per 1000 ppl in LA / Park acreage per 1000 ppl in other high-density US cities
Loss of CTS population as of 2002 due to habitat loss in LA
6.6 Acres

Total Percentage
Current Percentage
Biodiversity Budgets (Total $110M)
Pervious surfaces
1.2%
62.0%
73.0%
Historical change in wetland areas

- Interstitial
- Water
- Golf Course
- Parks
- Preserves

Key Species Research: California Tiger Salamander

Map Key

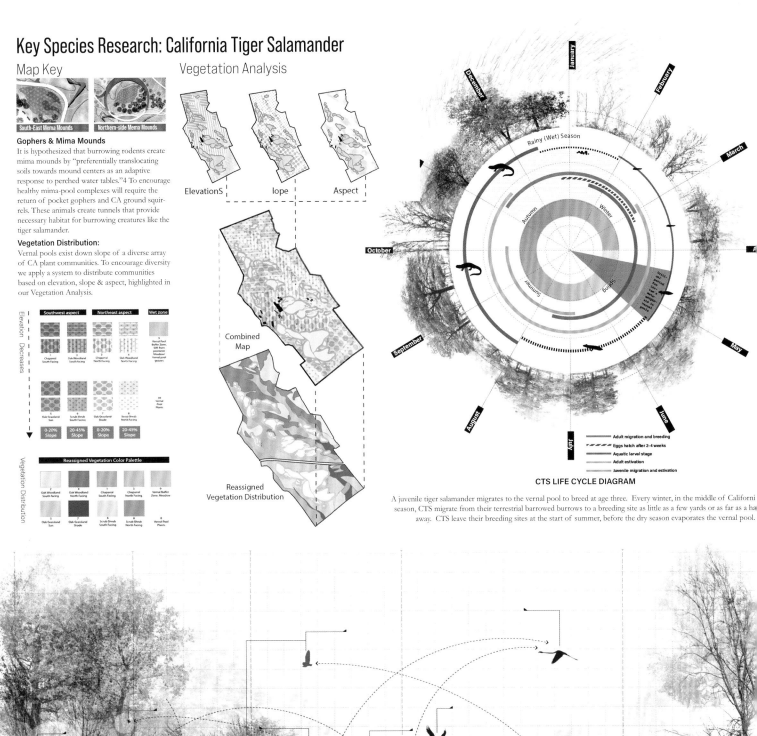

South-East Mema Mounds Northern-side Mema Mounds

Gophers & Mima Mounds

It is hypothesized that burrowing rodents create mima mounds by "preferentially translocating soils towards mound centers as an adaptive response to perched water tables."[4] To encourage healthy mima-pool complexes will require the return of pocket gophers and CA ground squirrels. These animals create tunnels that provide necessary habitat for burrowing creatures like the tiger salamander.

Vegetation Distribution:

Vernal pools exist down slope of a diverse array of CA plant communities. To encourage diversity we apply a system to distribute communities based on elevation, slope & aspect, highlighted in our Vegetation Analysis.

Elevation Decreases

Southwest aspect	Northeast aspect	Wet zone
Chaparral South-Facing	Chaparral North-Facing	Vernal Pool Buffer Zone, Soft Burn perimeter Meadow/ Vernal pool grasses
Oak Woodland South-Facing	Oak Woodland North-Facing	
Oak Grassland Sun	Oak Grassland Shade	Hi Vernal Pool Plants
Scrub Shrub South-Facing	Scrub Shrub North-Facing	
0-20% Slope	20-45% Slope	

Vegetation Distribution

Reassigned Vegetation Color Palette

Oak Woodland South facing / Oak Woodland North Facing / Chaparral South facing / Chaparral North Facing / Vernal Buffer Zone, Meadow / Oak Grassland Sun / Oak Grassland Shade / Scrub Shrub South Facing / Scrub Shrub North Facing / Vernal Pool Plants

Vegetation Analysis

ElevationS   lope   Aspect

Combined Map

Reassigned Vegetation Distribution

CTS LIFE CYCLE DIAGRAM

Rainy (Wet) Season

January, February, March, May, June, July, August, September, October, December

Autumn, Winter, Summer, Spring

Adult migration and breeding
Eggs hatch after 2-4 weeks
Aquatic larval stage
Adult estivation
Juvenile migration and estivation

A juvenile tiger salamander migrates to the vernal pool to breed at age three. Every winter, in the middle of Californi season, CTS migrate from their terrestrial barrowed burrows to a breeding site as little as a few yards or as far as a ha away. CTS leave their breeding sites at the start of summer, before the dry season evaporates the vernal pool.

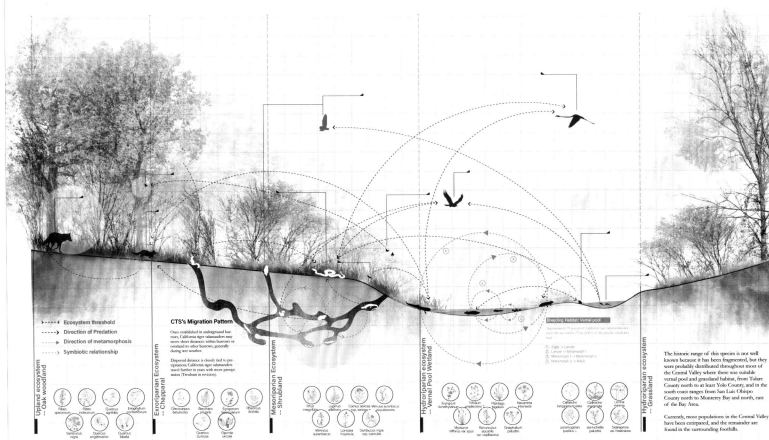

Ecosystem threshold
Direction of Predation
Direction of metamorphosis
Symbiotic relationship

CTS's Migration Pattern

Once established in underground burrows, California tiger salamanders may move short distances within burrows or overland to other burrows, generally during wet weather.

Dispersal distance is closely tied to precipitation; California tiger salamanders travel further in years with more precipitation (Trenham in revision).

Upland ecosystem -- Oak woodland

Exroriparian Ecosystem -- Chaparral

Mesoriparian Ecosystem -- Shrubland

Hydroriparian ecosystem -- Vernal Pool Wetland

Breeding Habitat: Vernal pool

Egg → Larvae
Larvae → Metamorph 1
Metamorph 1 → Metamorph 2
Metamorph 2 → Adult

Hydroriparian ecosystem -- Grassland

The historic range of this species is not well known because it has been fragmented, but they were probably distributed throughout most of the Central Valley where there was suitable vernal pool and grassland habitat, from Tulare County north to at least Yolo County, and in the south coast ranges from San Luis Obispo County north to Monterey Bay and north, east of the Bay Area.

Currently, most populations in the Central Valley have been extirpated, and the remainder are found in the surrounding foothills.

Seasonal Vernal Pools & Planting Scheme

European elder (sambucus nigra)

Mema Mound

Lemonade berry (rhus integrifolia)

Seating Area

Mesa Mint
(Pogogyne nudiuscula)

Great Egret

longstock water-starwort
(Callitriche longipedunculata)

California Tiger Salamander

Paths

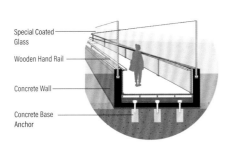

Special Coated Glass

Wooden Hand Rail

Concrete Wall

Concrete Base Anchor

Submerged Path Construction Details

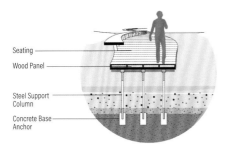

Seating

Wood Panel

Steel Support Column

Concrete Base Anchor

Boardwalk Construction Details

Planting Scheme Temporal Diagram

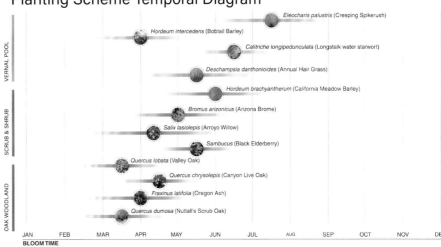

VERNAL POOL

Eleocharis palustris (Creeping Spikerush)
Hordeum intercedens (Bobtail Barley)
Calitriche longipedunculata (Longstalk water starwort)
Deschampsia danthonioides (Annual Hair Grass)
Hordeum brachyantherum (California Meadow Barley)

SCRUB & SHRUB

Bromus arizonicus (Arizona Brome)
Salix lasiolepis (Arroyo Willow)
Sambucus (Black Elderberry)

OAK WOODLAND

Quercus lobata (Valley Oak)
Quercus chrysolepis (Canyon Live Oak)
Fraxinus latifolia (Oregon Ash)
Quercus dumosa (Nuttall's Scrub Oak)

JAN FEB MAR APR MAY JUN JUL AUG SEP OCT NOV DEC
BLOOM TIME

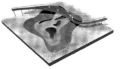

WET SEASON
November-February: Both shallow and deep vernal pools are filled with water. Primary vegetative growth.

BLOOM SEASON
March-June: Outer ring of vernal pools covered with showy flowerbed previously submerged in water.

DRY SEASON
July-October: Water level drops, pond-bed exposed; Autumn foliage refreshes the color palette of the area.

Marsilea vestita | Eleocharis macrostachya | Juncus bufonius | Juncus sphaerocarpus | Lilaea scilloides | Eleocharis acicularis | Hydrophilic Plants Wetland Riparian Plants | Callitriche marginata | Zannichellia palustris | Potamogeton pusillus L. | Lemna minima | Callitriche longiped uniculata | Hydrophilic Plants Wetland Riparian Plants | Marsilea vestita | Eleocharis macrostachya | Juncus bufonius | Juncus sphaerocarpus | Lilaea scilloides | Eleocharis acicularis

Ecological Corridor & Wildlife Crossing

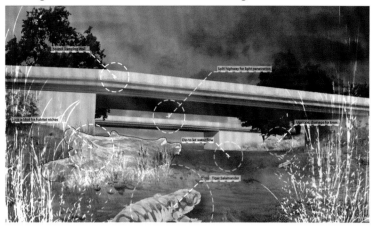

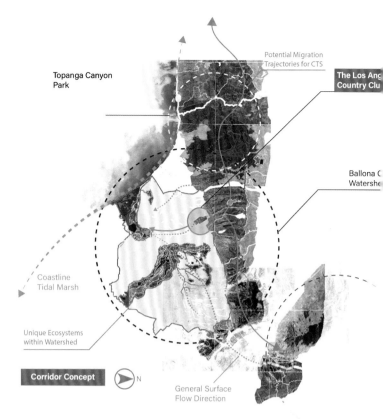

Topanga Canyon Park

Potential Migration Trajectories for CTS

The Los Ang Country Clu

Ballona C Watershe

Coastline Tidal Marsh

Unique Ecosystems within Watershed

Corridor Concept ⊙ N

General Surface Flow Direction

Animal vs Human Paths

Human Paths
Animal Paths
Boardwalks

Modification to Overhead Highway Structure
(Perspective of a crawling CTS)

To separate human & animal paths we propose building two tunnels. One 80 ft wide tunnel for animal use & a 30ft wide tunnel for human use. The two tunnels will cross under Wilshire Blvd, a busy four lane road & an underwhelming pedestrian sidewalk.

The topography around the animal tunnel will be mounded & planted with trees to obscure the animal entrance from human views. To increase vegetation and a diversity of nooks and crannies, Wilshire Blvd will be split into two smaller roads, creating a 40 ft opening. Walls will be added to this section of the road to decrease sound pollution within the tunnel.

Alternatively, the human tunnel will allow for a wide array of tunnel programs that connects seamlessly to human paths. The aim of this tunnel is to increase empathetic connection to burrowing species. Sensor data gathered from the animal tunnel will be projected onto various surfaces of the human tunnel to create an array of interactive experiences. Floor patterns & color will derive from CA vegetation patterns. The resulting tunnel will encourage intuitive learning of the complexity of burrowing habitats

The Los Angeles County Golf Club is situated between the Ballona Creek Watershed (south) and the Santa Monica Mountain Preserve (north). Conversion of the LACC golf course could be an initial step in creating a stepping stone habitat between these two preserves. We propose that other golf courses and cemetaries within this area could encourage future species migrations between the last few land preserves in Los Angeles.

Tunnel Construction Details

Fencing
Traffic Flow -----
Human/Animal Flow ——

Longitudinal Section Along Wilshire Blvd

— Oak woodland and Chaparral
— Vehicular Roadway

Additional trees planted to decrease view onto animal underpass
Animal Underpass

Ⓐ.

Human Underpass

Short Sections Along Human Paths

| Open Lawn | Path | Oak Woodlands & Chaparral | Oak Woodlands & Chaparral | Path | Vernal Pool | Mima Mounds | Path | Vernal Pool | Upland | Path | Pool | Path | Pool | Upland | Vernal Pool | Path | Vernal Pool | Oak Woodlands & Chaparral | Path | Oak Woodlands & Chaparral |

Ⓑ.   Ⓒ.   Ⓓ.   Ⓔ.   Ⓕ.   Ⓖ.

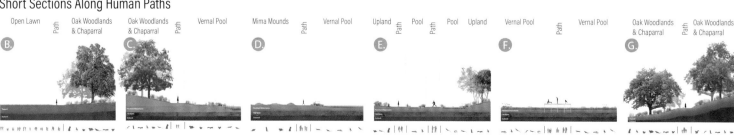

Underpass Sensory Interaction

Animal Tunnel Perspective

The animal tunnel is a rich array of California plants and non-vegetated surfaces, such as rocks, logs, and debris. These diverse array of materiality creates an abundant number of niches for tiger salamanders and other burrowing species to hide and feed while migrating between habitats.

Human Tunnel Perspective

This tunnel celebrates a wide array of California species and colors that are not only pleasant to look at but create a non-preachy educational experience that embraces both locality and complexity.

Sensory data gathered from the animal tunnel and vernal pool habitats can be projected into interactive forms for human use. This allows for humans to interact with tiger salamanders and other burrowing species without interupting their delicate life cycles.

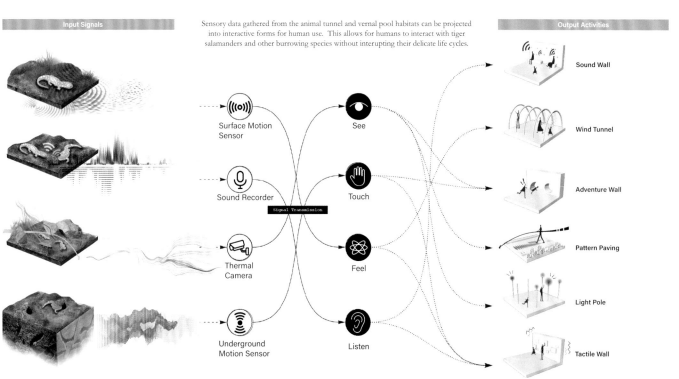

Citations

1. "The Ballona Wetlands: A Commitment to Current and Future Generations." Ballona Wetlands Restoration Project. Accessed October 20,2020. http://ballonarestoration.org/

2. John Strege. "LACC puts premium on privacy." ESPN. April 26, 2004. Accessed October 20, 2020. https://www.espn.com/golf/news/story?id=1790301

3. John Strege."A taxing issue for Los Angeles' equity clubs." Golf Digest: The Loop. July 17, 2010. Accessed October 20, 2020. https://www.golfdigest.com/story/a-taxing-issue-for-los-angeles-equity-clubs

4. Reeds and R. Amundson. "Sediment, gophers and time: a model for the origin and persistence of mima mound—vernal pool topography in the Great Central Valley." Studies from the Herbarium, Number 14. (2007): Pages 15-27. https://vernalpools.ucmerced.edu/sites/vernalpools.ucmerced.edu/files/documents/mima_mounds_vernal_pools_reed_amundson.pdf

5. G. Hammerson. 2004-09-10 "Ambystoma californiense, California Tiger Salamander." NatureServe Explorer. Published September 9, 2010. Accessed October 20, 2020. https://explorer.natureserve.org/Taxon/ELEMENT_GLOBAL.2.104488/Ambystoma_californiensece

FERAS ABDALLAH CALLA ROSE OSTRANDER

NORTH AMERICAN BEAVER
Castor canadensis

The American West is experiencing the most severe megadrought in human history. In a few years, if nothing is done, the Colorado River will run dry. This landscape, over-trapped and over-grazed, has been transformed from lush valley floors and wide river plains into defunct incised streams, disconnecting waterways from their respective floodplains and leaving bare, dusty desert. A human misconception led us to believe that industrial-scale engineering projects were needed to "tame" the "wild west" and bring European agricultural systems to what settlers saw as barren lands. The resulting mega-dams have perpetuated a false sense of water security. Water policies like "first come, first served" and "use it or lose it" have fostered a culture that aims to dominate and control nature, rather than one that seeks to cultivate relationships that thrive with it.

An unlikely mentor for forging symbiotic relationships with cohabiters, and arguably the greatest landscape architect of Turtle Island, the North American Beaver has historically stewarded riparia and the mall water cycles that hydrate the western landscape. Hunted almost to extinction for their pelts, beavers bring great value. They create conditions that enrich the soil, build robust wildlife habitat, and reverse the effects of aquifer depletion by raising the surrounding water table. Working with ranchers, rangers, farmers, and local populations, the installation of beaver dam analogs combined with holistic grazing management, will help reestablish suitable homes for beavers who slow the waters, rehydrating the landscape.

Solutions to degraded lands lie in physical intervention guided by empathy and a spirit of collaborative cohabitation with those that support the interrelated natural processes that shape the land. Supporting the presence of beavers in the landscape will help beavers rebuild the fundamentals that support human presence in the arid and semi-arid lands of the western United States.

THE NORTH AMERICAN BEAVER
CASTOR CANADENSIS

THE FUR TRADE

The Hudson's Bay Company, a fur-trading enterprise began operations, initiating the start of the American Fur Trade. Their largest export was beaver pelts.

FUR DESERT

"Made beaver" is treated as a form of currency. This encouraged trapper's to implement a fur desert policy that led to the overtrapping of beaver from their native landscape.

LAND CULTIVATION

Brigham Young arrives at Salt Lake and starts altering the land for crop cultivation. Wetland ecosystems are substituted for irrigation canals and ditches.

WESTWARD EXPANSION

The Desert Land Act was passed promoting the economic development of arid and semiarid public lands of the Western states. Thousands began migrating west, large scale agriculture ensued.

WATER POLITICS

The Reclamation Act paves the way for industrial scale engineering projects. Dams, irrigation canals and ditches strip the Colorado River of its natural flows, creating competition over water rights.

GRAZING PUBLIC LANDS

The Taylor Grazing Act allowed for grazing of public lands. Over-grazing of riparian ecosystems further degraded waterways, making it difficult for beavers to maintain freshwater resources.

ENGINEERED WATER

Colorado River Storage Act authorizes construction of major dam and reservoir projects throughout the river basins. This was a result of the Colorado River Compact, which divvied up water resources among the Western states.

RIVER RUNS DRY

The Colorado River, which 45 million people rely on for drinking water runs dry. This launches the utilization of beaver restoration techniques at the ecoregional scale.

REGENERATION

Beaver and human have fostered a symbiotic relationship, working together to be stewards of the land, biodiversity, and it's fragile freshwater ecosystems.

UPPER BASIN

GREEN RIVER

SALT LAKE CITY

YAMPA RIVER

COLORADO RIVER

DENVER

LOWER BASIN

LAS VEGAS

GLEN CANYON DAM

SAN JUAN RIVER

SANTA FE

HOOVER DAM

LITTLE COLORADO RIVER

ALBUQUERQUE

LOS ANGELES

PHOENIX

SALT RIVER

SAN DIEGO

GILA RIVER

YUMA

TUCSON

MEXICO

GULF OF CALIFORNIA

MAJOR DAM +
RESERVOIR
URBAN AREA
WETLAND
WATERWAYS
GRAZING ALLOTMENT
BEAVER REINTRODUCTION O

RIPARIA

WILLOW

TREE PROTECTION

THE LODGE

SIDE CHANNEL

MAIN POND

EXISTING CONDITION

BEAVER DAM

PROPOSED CONDITION

Poor grazing management has stripped the land of its riparian vegetation. Without beaver to steward the waterways, stream incision and riverbank destabilization make the land highly prone to erosion. The water table drops and the land becomes void of moisture.

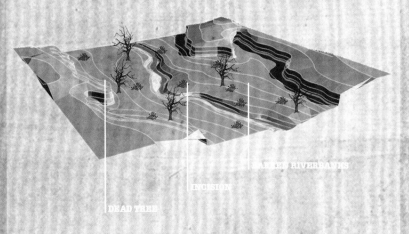

DEAD TREE

INCISION

BARREN RIVERBANKS

WATER TABLE

LOCAL AMBIENT TEMPERATURE — 105° F

CLIENT DESCRIPTION

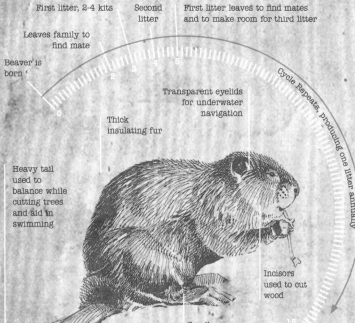

First litter, 2-4 kits
Second litter
First litter leaves to find mates and to make room for third litter

Leaves family to find mate

Beaver is born

Cycle Repeats, producing one litter annually

Transparent eyelids for underwater navigation

Thick insulating fur

Heavy tail used to balance while cutting trees and aid in swimming

Incisors used to cut wood

Small webbed feet

15 years

Beaver dam analogs are installed to support beaver dam building when the river is still prone to flash flooding. Rotational grazing and responsible land management allow for time for the river to start to heal.

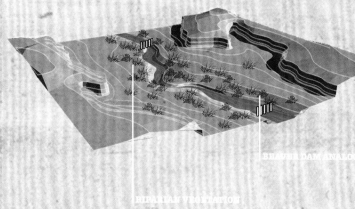

BEAVER DAM ANALOG

RIPARIAN VEGETATION

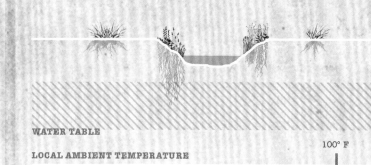

WATER TABLE

LOCAL AMBIENT TEMPERATURE — 100° F

FOOD CULTIVATION

WILLOW   CATTAILS   LEAVES

Beavers create conditions that support their vegetarian diet. They eat fast growing plants, small twigs, leaves, and aquatic vegetation.

SHELTER

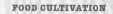

WATER

POND LODGE   BANK LODGE

Beavers need water to shelter from predators. They build shelter in two forms based off the current condition of the waterway

BUILDING MATERIALS

ROCKS   MUD   STICKS

Beaver use readily available natural building materials to construct dams and lodges.

SMALL WATER CYCLE

WATER FOLLOWS CARB

H20 → C

DAM   ROC

BEAVER   VEGETA

Beavers are experts at crea conditions that regenerate maintain damaged small wa Through dam building and plant cultivation, Carbon ge in the soil, thus allowing wa moisture to stick around. O family can store up to 3 gallons of water.

75 years

150 years

...vers are reintroduced to the landscape, building dams and side channels to broaden the ...'s capacity to hold water. A main pond is formed behind the dam, where the beavers live. ...rian vegetation returns to the riverbanks now that water is accessible to plant roots.

The valley floor becomes a braided riparian ecosystem. Temperatures drop and the small water cycle is rehabilitated, providing conditions that sustain a diversity of flora and fauna. Trees begin to come back, further enhancing a microclimate that brings rain to the landscape.

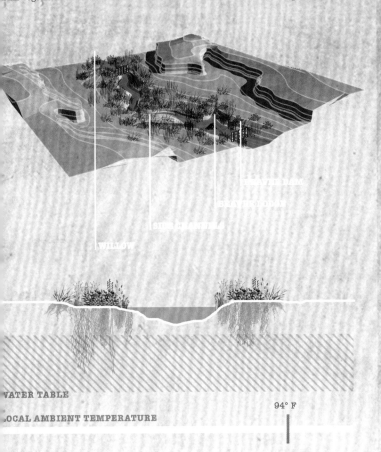

WILLOW
SIDE CHANNEL
BEAVER DAM
BEAVER DAM

WATER TABLE

LOCAL AMBIENT TEMPERATURE   94° F

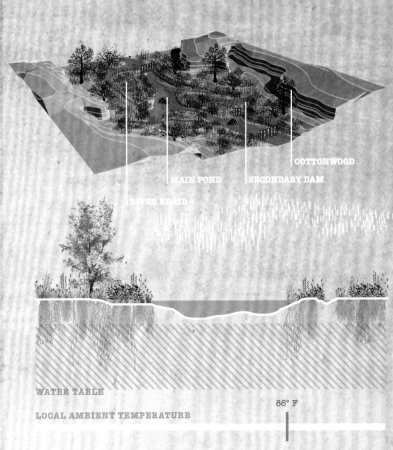

COTTONWOOD
MAIN POND
SECONDARY DAM
RIVER BRAID

WATER TABLE

LOCAL AMBIENT TEMPERATURE   86° F

...ANAGEMENT STRATEGIES

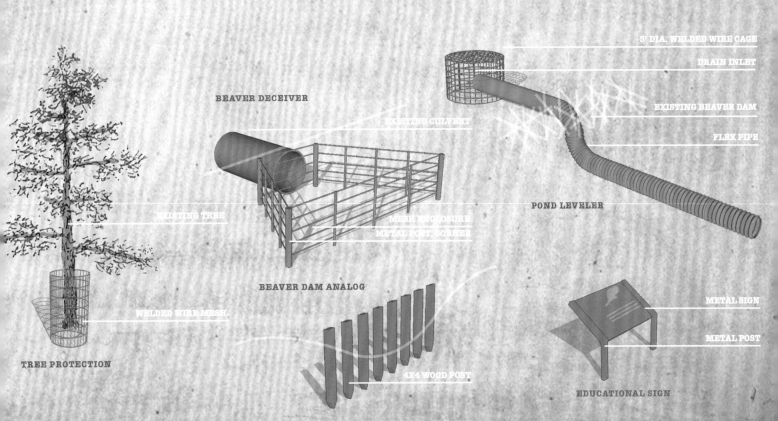

TREE PROTECTION
EXISTING TREE
WELDED WIRE MESH

BEAVER DECEIVER
EXISTING CULVERT
MESH ENCLOSURE
METAL POST, CORNER
BEAVER DAM ANALOG
4X4 WOOD POST

5' DIA. WELDED WIRE CAGE
DRAIN INLET
EXISTING BEAVER DAM
FLEX PIPE
POND LEVELER

METAL SIGN
METAL POST
EDUCATIONAL SIGN

NATIVE LANDS

The American West was historically inhabited by Native tribes who fostered a relationship with the native landscape. The North American Beaver, "The Sacred Center" as they called it, has tremendous ability to create and maintain riparian ecosystems, alleviating drought by keeping moisture in local circulation.

THE INDUSTRIAL COMPLEX

As settlers colonize western lands, they bring with them a practice of over-extraction. Industrial scale engineering projects are built to sustain industrial scale agriculture. Monoculture cultivation, overtilling, and over-grazing laid waste to riparian ecosystems, ultimately leading to the worst drought in human history.

THE TRAPPER'S TRAIL

As beaver pelts became a European commodity, The Hudson Bay Company and "Mountain Men" ventured west to trap the animal. This led to the near extinction of the North American Beaver. Ironically, their Fur desert policy which aimed to sabotage competitors would initiate the process of desertification.

By halting the practice of over-grazing and over-extraction, beavers are reintroduced to tend to the waterways they once occupied. The return of riparia is attributed to the fruition of responsible land and water management. The land is healing and making way for moisture to stay in a once barren landscape.

BINGJIAN LIU ESTHER JUNG HEEJUNG SHIN

AMERICAN EEL
Anguilla rostrata

American eels are known to be mysterious nocturnal creatures. They spawn in remote and nutrient-poor places in the seas, and are rarely visible to people. However, what many people don't realize about eels is that they are migratory fish that travel long distances from oceans to small creeks, and eventually return to the ocean where they spawn and die. Even though eels are known to have a significant role in the aquatic ecosystem, their populations are plummeting. American, Japanese, and European eels have become scarce, with populations dropping by more than 90% in the past four decades. Restoration of eel populations is difficult unless we tackle the list of contributors to their decline: loss of habitat, dam blockage, fishing, pollutants, and changes in ocean currents. These factors make eel population management problematic.

This design focuses on New York's Hudson River where industrialization and human activities have caused many hindrances in eel migration, as well as loss of their habitats. The project consists of two parts. Part one, the "eel oasis," creates habitat modules for eels on different parts of the Hudson River and tributaries where the ecosystem has become non-functional. These modules feature buoyant plastic reefs and limbs made of recycled plastics that offer eels a place to hide and rest on their migration path. Part two involves the construction of "eel ladders" on dams where glass eels (early stage eels) have trouble using existing fish ladders. Together, the oases and ladders facilitate the eels' long migration journey toward deeper creeks and smaller streams. In addition, these modules also serve as walkable trails for people to increase awareness of the eels' presence and benefits to the aquatic ecosystem.

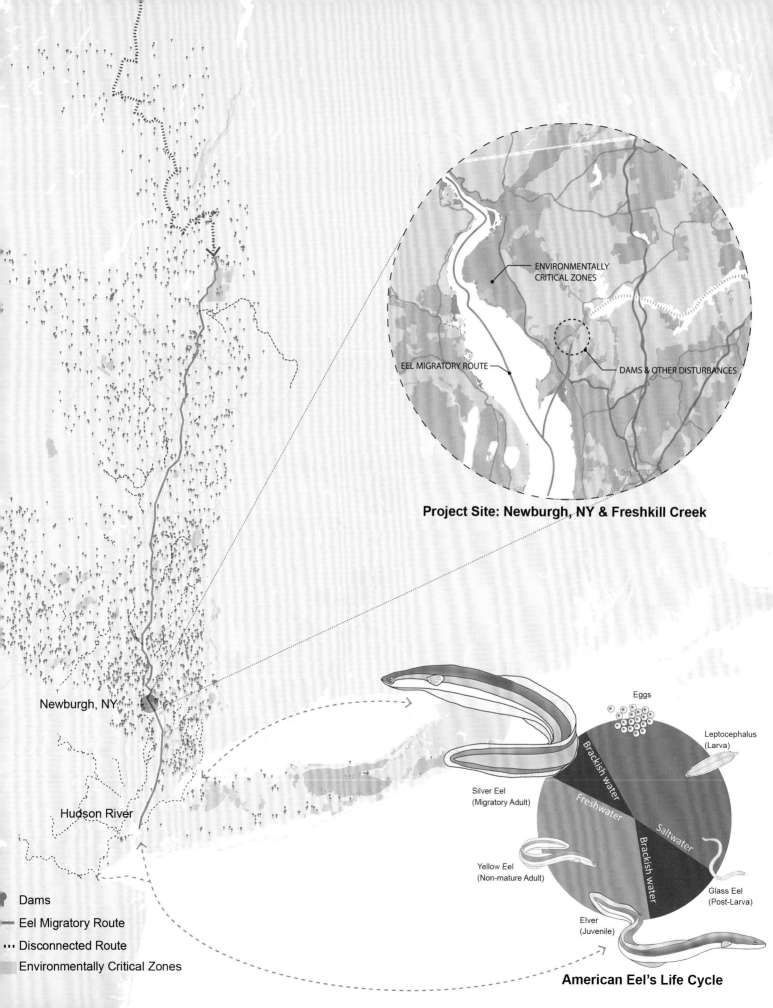

Project Site: Newburgh, NY & Freshkill Creek

ENVIRONMENTALLY
CRITICAL ZONES

EEL MIGRATORY ROUTE

DAMS & OTHER DISTURBANCES

Newburgh, NY

Hudson River

Dams

Eel Migratory Route

Disconnected Route

Environmentally Critical Zones

Eggs

Leptocephalus
(Larva)

Silver Eel
(Migratory Adult)

Brackish water

Freshwater

Saltwater

Brackish water

Yellow Eel
(Non-mature Adult)

Glass Eel
(Post-Larva)

Elver
(Juvenile)

American Eel's Life Cycle

EEL OASIS: New Habitats on Migratory Route

50ft

15 ft

EEL MIGRATING ROUTE

FISHKILL

BEACON

NEWBURGH

The eel oasis, composed of connected floating modules along the shores of the Hudson River, improves the migration route with more rest stops for the eels. These modules create a shaded, hospitable underwater environment, which conforms to the favorable environment of eels. The oasis could also provide public space for humans in the adjacent urban area.

esigned for All Sizes

ferent types of dams have built over
e along the tributaries of the Hudson
ver. These dams obstruct eels along
h other migratory fish to travel upward
vards smaller streams and creeks where
ey stay most of their life. Eel ladder is
signed to facilitate even small glass eel
pass through different sizes of dams.

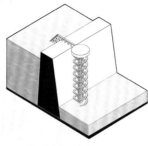

High Head Dam

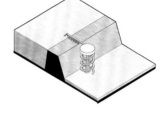

Medium Head Dam

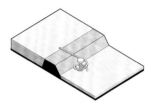

Low Head Dam

nimpeded Paths for Young Eels

aterflow

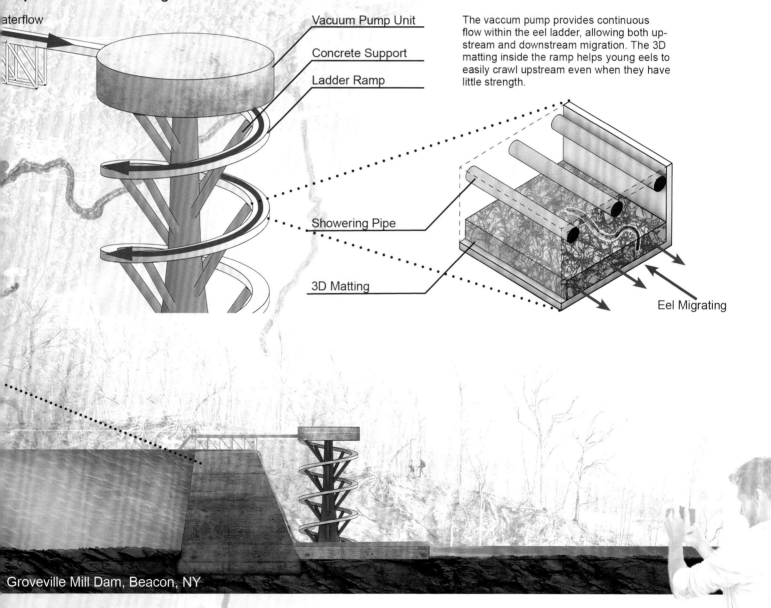

Vacuum Pump Unit

Concrete Support

Ladder Ramp

Showering Pipe

3D Matting

The vaccum pump provides continuous
flow within the eel ladder, allowing both upstream and downstream migration. The 3D
matting inside the ramp helps young eels to
easily crawl upstream even when they have
little strength.

Eel Migrating

Groveville Mill Dam, Beacon, NY

EEL OASIS MODULE

Wetland Module

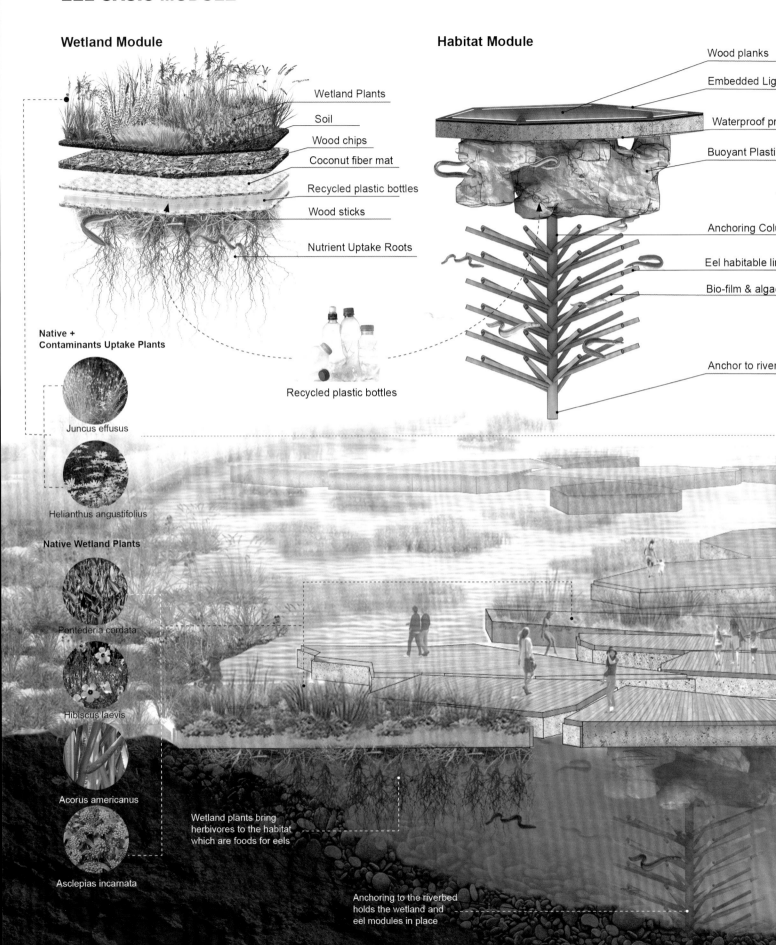

Wetland Plants
Soil
Wood chips
Coconut fiber mat
Recycled plastic bottles
Wood sticks
Nutrient Uptake Roots

**Native +
Contaminants Uptake Plants**

Juncus effusus

Helianthus angustifolius

Native Wetland Plants

Pontederia cordata

Hibiscus laevis

Acorus americanus

Asclepias incarnata

Recycled plastic bottles

Habitat Module

Wood planks
Embedded Lig
Waterproof pr
Buoyant Plasti
Anchoring Col
Eel habitable li
Bio-film & alga
Anchor to river

Wetland plants bring
herbivores to the habitat
which are foods for eels

Anchoring to the riverbed
holds the wetland and
eel modules in place

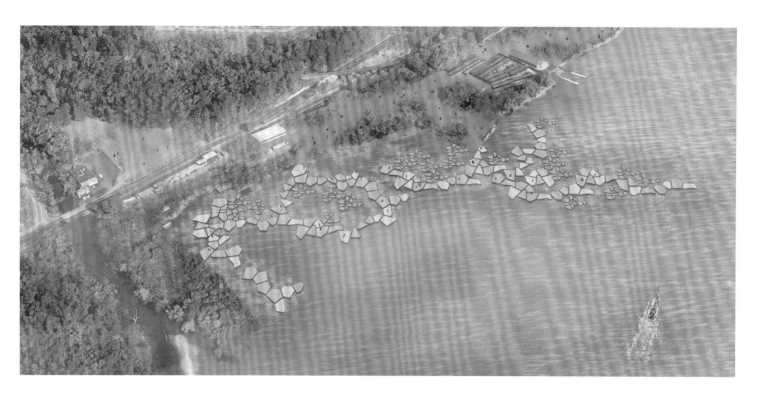

Plastic reef and limbs
create dark and hospitable
conditions for eels

ARTHUR LAM

BIRDS
Aves spp.

Birds have long been considered sacred in various cultures, acting as both the bridge between heaven and Earth, as well as symbols of hope and freedom. In spite of the important role they play in our lives, many of our actions are detrimental to their survival. As a result of anthropogenic climate change and build-up of dead trees in forests, the recent mega-fires in California have wreaked havoc at an unprecedented scale, ridding many native avian species of their food and shelter. Although it was once true that many forests and their ecosystems would regrow stronger following a forest fire, the same can no longer be said given the current environmental state of our planet.

With birds being some of nature's most effective seed dispersers and exterminators, the intent of this design is to create a temporary safe haven for birds to return to so that they may facilitate the regrowth of their natural home. This can be achieved through the construction of a modular simulation of their natural environment. With regard to materiality and spatial quality, the primary structure mimics the scaffolding branches of a tree. Using the knowledge we have about these creatures, ideal spaces intended for private and public use can then be plugged into the scaffolding structure to provide birds with shelter, food, and plenty of seeds to disperse. Not only does this design aim to restore the ecological balance of the land, but it moreover strives to shed light on the critical role that these beautiful creatures play and the wonders that they can achieve.

Nest boxes are
oriented towards the northeast
and southeast to shelter inhabitants
from the westerly winds of California.

Interior Condition

Worm's Eye

1/16"=1'0" 0   5   10   15   20   25 FT

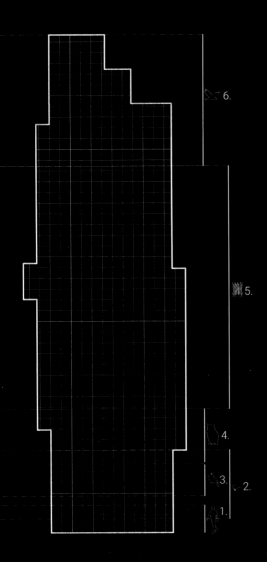

6.

5.

4.

3.
2.

1.

3. Open Nester Dwelling

Nest Box Specifications:
Occupiable space: 8"x8"x8"
Height above ground level: 8'-15'
Entrance Hole: None

Accommodated Species
American Robin, Scrub jay, Oriole, etc.

Feature:
The lack of an entrance hole provides
these birds with a free and open environment.

4. Cavity Nester Dwelling

Nest Box Specifications:
Occupiable space: 6"x6"x12"
Height above ground level:15'-28'
Entrance Hole: 2.5" radius at 9" above the base

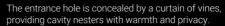

Accommodated Species
Flicker, Screech Owl, Kestrel, etc.

Feature:
The entrance hole is concealed by a curtain of vines,
providing cavity nesters with warmth and privacy.

5a. Public Space: Shaded Bird Bath

Bath Specifications:
Occupiable space: 2'-3" radius x 3" depth

Height above ground level: 28"-80'

Accommodated Species
Small Birds, Open Nesters, and
Cavity Nesters

5b. Public Space: Large Planters

Planter Specifications:
Occupiable space: 3.5'x2.5'

Height above ground level: 28"-80'

Accommodated Species
Primarily Small Birds and Open Nesters

1. Human Occupation

Ground level shelters serve as storage
spaces for simple reforestation
equipment as well as contemplative rest
spots for human visitors.

2. Small Bird Dwelling

Nest Box Specifications:
Occupiable space: 4.5"x4.5"x8"
Height above ground level: 3'-25'
Entrance Hole: 1.2" radius at 6" above the base

Accommodated Species
Black Capped Chickadee, Blue bird, Swallow,
Pygmy Nuthatch, etc.

Feature:
The tops of the dwellings are relatively flat, allowing for shared
spaces to easily be formed for these sociable creatures.

6. Large Bird Dwelling

Nest Platform Specifications:
Occupiable space: 6'x6'
Height above ground level: 80'-115'
Entrance Hole: None

Accommodated Species
Bald Eagle, Red-tailed, Hawk, Large Owls, etc.

Feature:
Platforms are open to the sky and provide a
panoramic view of the surrounding environment.

Shading Elements

Much like leaves in a tree, the perforated cloth shades provide a seemingly stochastic environment within the structure.

Habitable Space

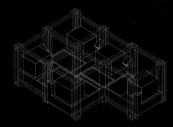

Joint members form micro-communities from individual units, allowing for previously unfound relationships to be established between different species.

Scaffolding Structure

The primary structure is constructed from recycled 2"x2" lumber. Not only does it act as a receptor for habitable spaces, but these branch-like structures also allow for inhabitants to perch and rest on them.

HONORABLE

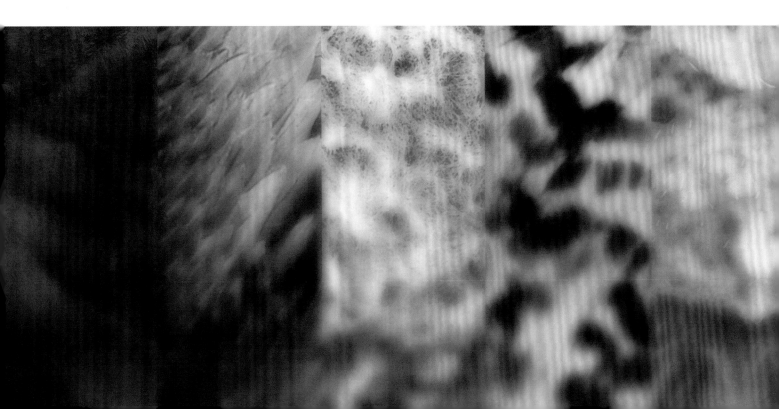

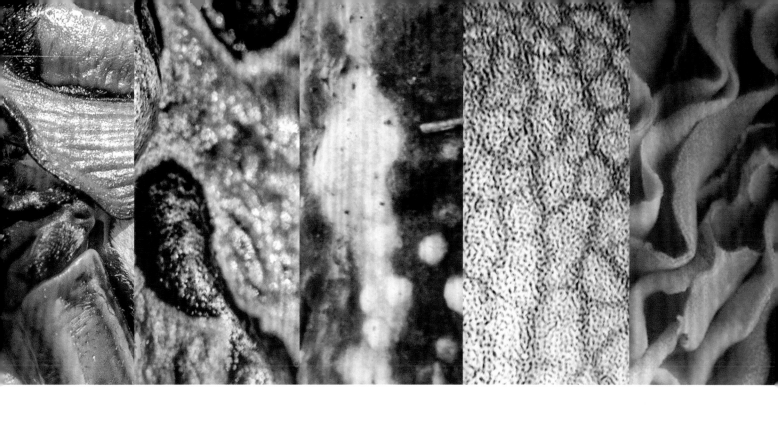

MENTIONS

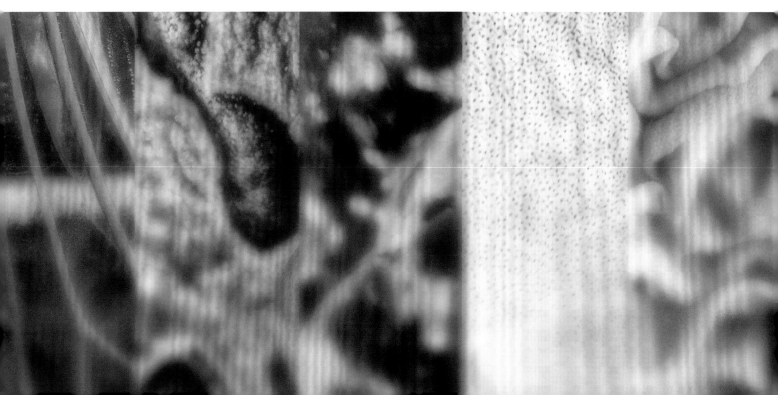

MARZIA MICALI

COMMON OCTOPUS *Octopus vulgaris*

The octopus is a mysterious animal, the subject of myths, legends, and tales of sea monsters, especially in the Mediterranean. Cefalù, Sicily–the chosen site for this project–has a strong relationship between land and water, carrying the legacy of the island kraken, an ancient myth where the body of the kraken sea monster was thought of as an island, despite its tentacles flitting about the dark waters below. This monstrous portrayal is in contrast with its real vulnerability, a vulnerability heightened since the loss of its shell during the Cretaceous period.

The aim of this project is to create a connection between land and water matching the animal's need for shelter with human's vulnerability on the water. Referencing recent studies on the behavior of octopuses' aggregate colonies, the design is for an octopuses' garden. The project's title, "Imprinting," comes from the idea of creating a dialogue between humans and octopuses, exploring this term in both of its meanings: to impress or stamp a mark on a surface, and to attach by recognizing another animal or thing as an entity of habitual trust. Each species has its own object, linked together by a series of delicate cables tethering the seabed to the surface. Octopus houses are concrete blocks with interior sections that they can use to hide, camouflage, hunt, play, and contribute to a new ecosystem thanks to the debris and shells they collect. On the surface there is a platform designed to bring humans to the animal – connecting tidal motion to the habitat below and holding the underwater world and the surface world together.

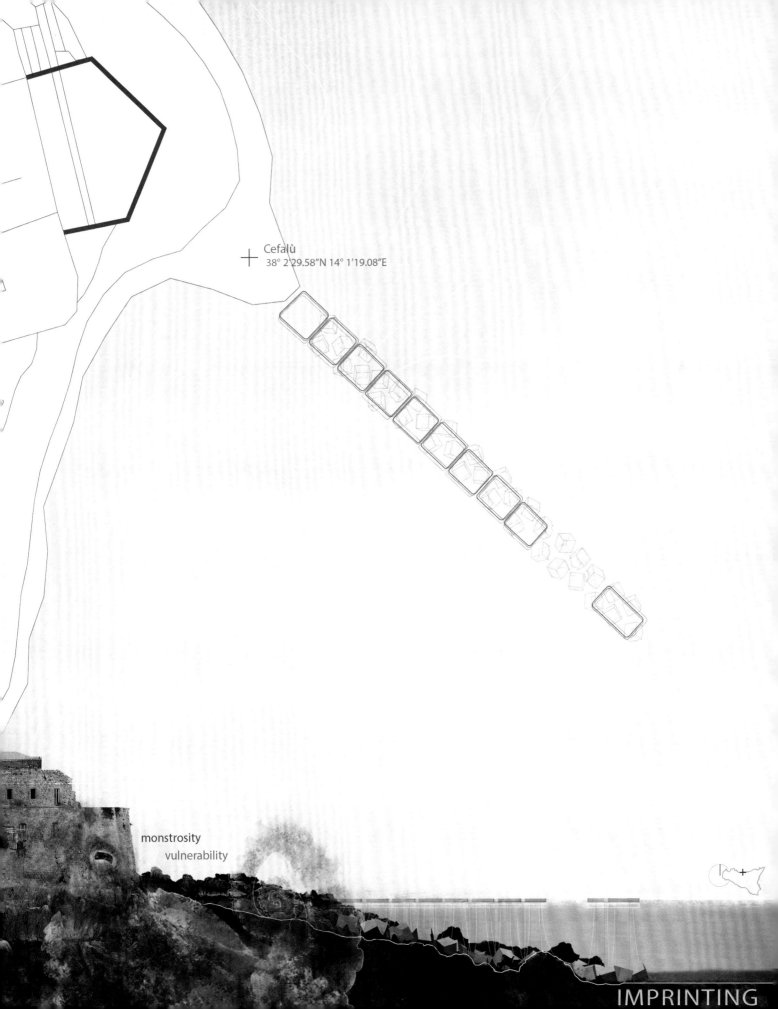

Cefalù
38° 2'29.58"N 14° 1'19.08"E

monstrosity
vulnerability

IMPRINTING

moving platforms

the octopus garden

ecosystem from debris

relationships

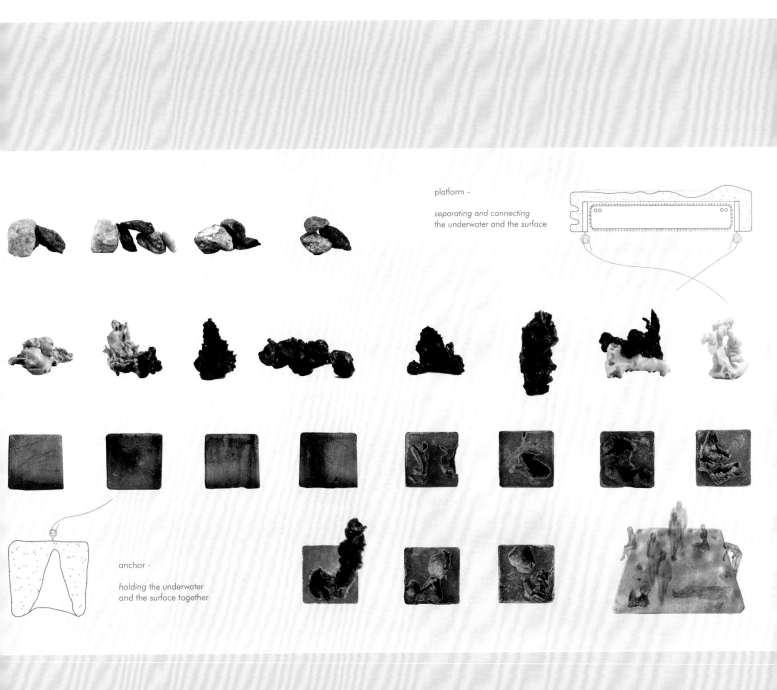

platform -

separating and connecting
the underwater and the surface

anchor -

holding the underwater
and the surface together

ZHOU WANG

PACIFIC WALRUS *Odobenus rosmarus divergens*

The migration of the Pacific walrus is seriously impeded by the rapid disappearance of sea ice in the Arctic area caused by global warming. Female and young walruses chase the sea ice every year for their food and fresh water supply; however, it is becoming increasingly difficult for walruses to find sea ice in summer so they desperately gather on the small ice packs or are stranded on the land causing hundreds of deaths. This proposal aims to help walruses migrate by providing them with a suitable northward migration route and by building conveyors to help them find the nearest sea ice annually to face the global warming challenge. This is particularly crucial for the young walruses confronted with ever-lengthening migrations that may be beyond their capabilities.

The migration strategy has three stages to deal with remaining sea ice at different times. The conveyor, with its ice surface, will help the walruses travel the long distances now required to reach the retreating sea ice. The conveyor features a cooling system to keep the ice surface frozen powered by sea-current turbines underneath the platform that produce renewable energy. The conveyors will be organized as a fleet and connected by a tugboat, requiring a human team to manage the operation. The tugboat also functions as an observer to monitor the walruses and share the activity with the public. The walrus migration mission presents a great opportunity to share the lives of marine animals in the beautiful Arctic landscape and to increase human empathy by bringing attention to endangered Arctic animals.

PACIFIC WALRUS REFUGEE MISSION

Dying walrus

Disappearing sea ice

KEYWORD
Requirement for habitat: shallow water, sea ice
Food: bentho community
Predator: polar bear, whale
Other facts: social animal, hunted by human

MIGRATION ROUTE

Stage 3
2050 – ?

No more sea ice in Chukchi Sea, sea ice only happens near Greenland. Pacific walruses will live in Greenland forever unless they adapt to the ice-free environment.

Stage 2
2035-2050

Sea ice gradually retreats northward in summer. Walruses are conveyed to ice floes on both sides of the Bering Strait and are returned in the fall.

Stage 1
2020-2035

Ice floes still exist in the north Bering Strait in summer and grow southward in winter. The walrus conveyer will direct some groups of migrating walruses farther north to reduce pressure on limited resources.

Assisted migration

WALRUS REFUGEE MISSION
INTERNATIONAL CAMPAIGN

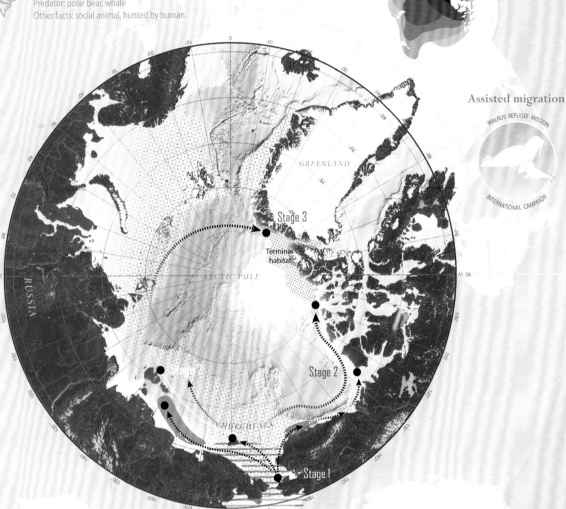

GREENLAND

Stage 3
Terminal habitat

ARCTIC POLE

RUSSIA

Stage 2

CHUKCHI SEA

Stage 1

BERING SEA

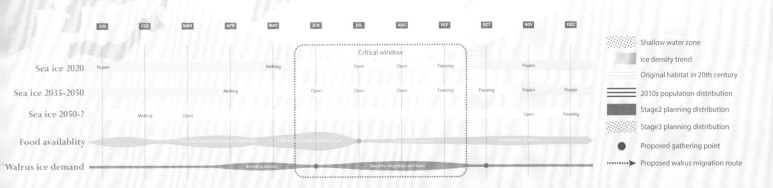

	JUN	FEB	MAR	APR	MAY	JUN	JUL	AUG	SEP	OCT	NOV	DEC
						Critical window						
Sea ice 2020	Frozen				Melting		Open	Open	Freezing		Frozen	
Sea ice 2035-2050			Melting			Open	Open	Open	Freezing	Freezing	Frozen	Frozen
Sea ice 2050-?		Melting	Open							Open	Freezing	
Food availablity												
Walrus ice demand					Breeding season		Need for migration and food					

Shallow water zone
Ice density trend
Original habitat in 20th century
2010s population distribution
Stage2 planning distribution
Stage3 planning distribution
● Proposed gathering point
┄┄┄► Proposed walrus migration route

WALRUS CONVEYOR

The conveyor seeks to help walruses migrate by providing them with a safe migration route and assisting them to reach sea ice that is retreating northward due to global warming.

1960-2000
Because of their huge girth, walrus are relatively clumsy in water. During their annual migration, they rely on large floating patches of ice as resting stops or mobile fishing platforms as they make their voyage cross the shallow frigid waters between Alaska and Russia.

10000-20000 walruses lives in Pacific Ocean in 20th century. The USGS put the chances of extinction or serious population decline among walrus at 40% by 2095 because of the rapid and widespread loss of summer sea ice due to warming temperatures.

Disappearing summer sea ice, due to climate change, is likely to spur an increase in shipping traffic through the Chukchi and Bering seas, putting the walruses in further jeopardy.

2050-?
The Pacific walrus will merge with the Atlantic walrus. There will be no significant physical differences between them, and Greenland will be the only place with sea ice in 100 years.

ASSISTED MIGRATION

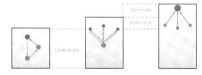

EXISTING INTERACTION WALRUS - SEA ICE

Curved surface

Cooling pipe

Floating block
(hollow air pocket)

Framework

Propeller

Sea current turbine

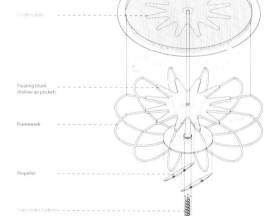

AGGREGATION

Connected with tugboat · Move to different direction · Sea current turbine

SECTION

SPRING - MELTING

sea current

Moving speed: 0 mph

FALL - MIGRATING

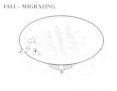

Moving speed: 2-6 mph

COOLING SYSTEM

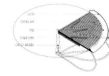

EARLY SUMMER - MOVING

Moving speed: 2-6 mph

WINTER - FREEZING

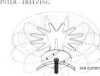

sea current

Moving speed: 0 mph

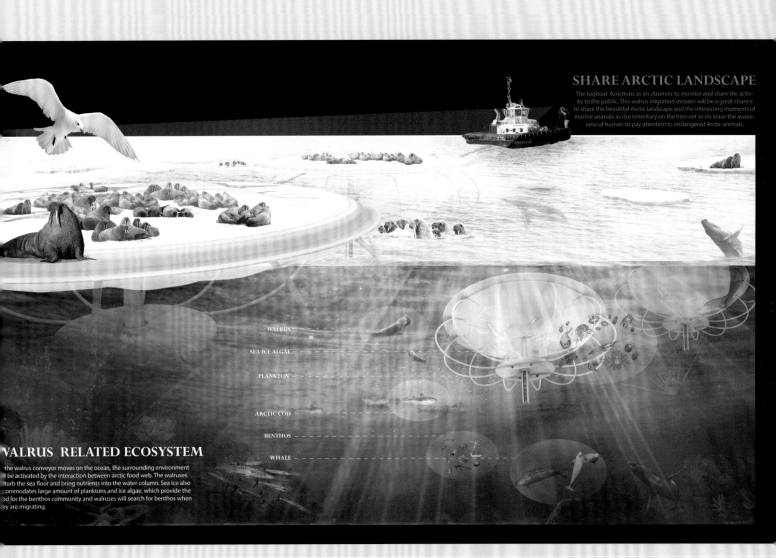

SHARE ARCTIC LANDSCAPE

The tugboat functions as an observer to monitor and share the activity to the public. This walrus migration mission will be a great chance to share the beautiful Arctic landscape and the interesting moments of marine animals as documentary on the Internet to increase the awareness of human to pay attention to endangered Arctic animals.

WALRUS

SEA ICE ALGAE

PLANKTON

ARCTIC COD

BENTHOS

WHALE

VALRUS RELATED ECOSYSTEM

the walrus conveyor moves on the ocean, the surrounding environment
be activated by the interaction between arctic food web. The walruses
turb the sea floor and bring nutrients into the water column. Sea ice also
ommodates large amount of planktons and ice algae, which provide the
d for the benthos community and walruses will search for benthos when
ey are migrating.

HILLARY DEWILDT

CALIFORNIA BROWN PELICAN *Pelecanus occidentalis californicus*

In 2009, amid enormous fanfare, the brown pelican was removed from the Endangered Species List. Since then, California brown pelicans–a slightly smaller version of the subspecies–have experienced unprecedented nesting failures and starvation due to overfishing of Pacific sardines, their most important food source. As fish stocks continue to decline, thousands of brown pelicans in southern California are at risk of starvation and death, which may lead to the relisting of this subspecies as endangered in the near future. The "Aviary" seeks to support these vulnerable marine birds by coupling new bird habitat with decommissioned offshore oil infrastructures.

Offshore oil rigs in southern California provide an important resting place for California brown pelicans during their migration south along the Pacific Flyway, with the birds flying from platform to platform as they make their way to Mexico. As these offshore rigs become decommissioned over the next 25 years they will leave behind remnant infrastructures, presenting a unique opportunity for marine habitat enhancement. Using the support structure of the decommissioned oil-drilling towers, the Aviary provides an alternative nesting ground for California brown pelicans with adequate space to roost, preen, land, and take off. Two wing-shaped exoskeletons wrap around the tower, partially enclosing the nesting ground. The artificial rookery provides multiple nesting platforms at varying heights, changing what is currently a makeshift habitat into an intentional habitat to ensure the safety of the California brown pelican for years to come. While only a relatively small step, the Aviary will breathe new life into the metal husks left behind by the Anthropocene age.

Proposed Decommissioning Plan
Platform "Holly"
SHEET 1 of 3   3-11-2021

SUN OIL COMPANY et al

OCS-P-0240   SSM Group
Ventura   California

500m Federal Marine Reserve Boundary

✕ 34.3899° N, 119.9064° W

TOPSIDE

Aviary

Decommissioned Drilling Rig

Main Deck

TOPSIDE
JACKET

EL. 0.0' M.L.L.W.

Fish Assemblages

Jacket Leg

JACKET

76
70
60
50
40
30
20
10
0
-10
-20
-30
-40
-50
-60
-70

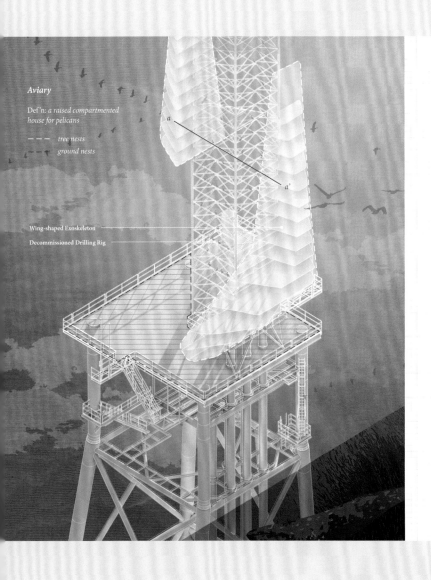

Aviary

Def'n: *a raised compartmented house for pelicans*

– – – *tree nests*
– · – · *ground nests*

Wing-shaped Exoskeleton
Decommissioned Drilling Rig

a
a'

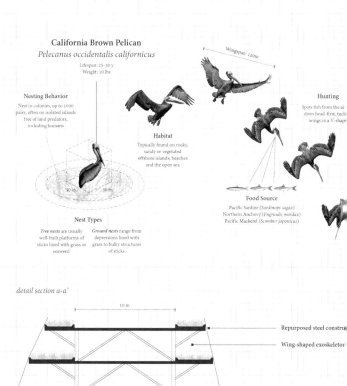

California Brown Pelican
Pelecanus occidentalis californicus

Lifespan: 25-30 y
Weight: 10 lbs

Wingspan: 120 in

Nesting Behavior

Nest in colonies, up to 1000 pairs, often on isolated islands free of land predators, including humans.

Habitat

Typically found on rocky, sandy or vegetated offshore islands, beaches and the open sea

Hunting

Spots fish from the air, dives head-first, tucking wings in a V-shape

30 in   30 in

Nest Types

Tree nests are usually well-built platforms of sticks lined with grass or seaweed

Ground nests range from depressions lined with grass to bulky structures of sticks

Food Source

Pacific Sardine (*Sardinops sagax*)
Northern Anchovy (*Engraulis mordax*)
Pacific Mackerel (*Scomber japonicus*)

detail section a-a'

10 m

Repurposed steel constru
Wing-shaped exoskeleto

Perches for landing and take-off

Nesting platforms at various heights for multiple bird families

*The **Aviary** redefines offshore oil infrastructures as productive components of the southern California landscape, enhancing its aesthetic qualities alongside its ecological potentials.*

Platform "Holly"

Southern California Bight

AROUSSIAK GABRIELIAN

SHIITAKE MUSHROOM *Lentinula edodes*

Rather than consider the creature as client–a term that implies a transactional relationship–I chose to imagine how humans might exist in beneficial and empathic mutuality with co-species, *Lentinula edodes* (shiitake mushroom). To facilitate this human-fungal collaboration, the design of "Transcorporeal Atmospheres" is an undulating vessel that collects human breath to create optimal conditions for *Letinula edodes* to thrive. Environmental philosopher David Macauley (*Elemental Philosophy*, 2010) reminds us that our "breath is routinely circulated and shared with others... We are conspiring–literally, breathing together–and to contemplate this fact can dramatically change our lives to reveal new ways that human others and nonhuman otherness are woven into the very elemental conditions of our existence."

Transcorporeal Atmospheres explores what it means to share our breath and the water it contains. The word atmosphere comes from the Greek *atmos* (vapor) and *sphaira* (ball). The project creates such a communal sphere of vapor as watershed for the survival and evolution of these fungal symbiont. It welcomes breathing as a communal action that collects airborne particles of water that we collectively inhale and release with the more-than-human world. The project gathers the waters of this communal exhale for hydration and nourishment of shiitake fungus which filters the water and magnifies its abundance by its own breath through the production of metabolic water (an ability unique to the shiitake). In response to increasing water scarcity, this amplified breathing system presents a new kind of hydrocommons that ensures co-survival. The designed system is not meant to create a closed loop, but over time will extend to supply water to other organisms that would become the co-inhabitants of this new emergent ecosystem. By tying oneself into networks of mutual exchange and codependence, this human-fungal assemblage inspires us to imagine a more compassionate and collaborative form of earthly inhabitation.

Developed in consultation with microbiologist and mycology expert Dr. Han Wosten, Utrecht University.

Transcorporeal Atmospheres

Transcorporeal Atmospheres aims to make palpable our planetary hydrocommons through a human-fungal assemblage. Humans are invited to press themselves into the depressions of the outer membrane and breathe into tubular mouthpieces. As the water from the breath passes though the fungus to enable its growth, the fungus filters the impurities in that liquid – "dehumanizing" the water in the process. Shiitake create surplus water through the metabolism of plant waste – known as metabolic water – which it subsequently exhales or excretes out of its body. This surplus water is transported into a centralized and communal cistern, gathering it for wider use within this symbiotic hydrocollective. The designed system is not meant to create a closed loop but over time will extend to supply water to other organisms that would become the co-inhabitants of this new emergent ecosystem.

Exterior application of designed system to facilliate human-fungal collaboration and the collective production of water for communal, multispecies use. Size of overall system varies and depends on the specificities of the site's context.

designed **system**

The system uses mycelium over a hardwood framework that faciliates the inoculation of the Shiitake mushroom. This base is formed to funnel accumulated water (from vapor) to the internal inoculation site (g) for the fungus which requires 80% shade. At this point, the water passing through the mushrooms is filtered before collection in the central cistern (h). Flexible 3D-printed mouthpieces (d) extend from the interior of the system and create a network of inner organs (c) that channel the cumulative water toward the base to nourish the Shiitake and other companion species. The outer surface (a) acts as a protective layer from wind and its undulation contains transpiration pods (b) that additionally collect moisture from the shiitake and other emergent co-species as they transpire.

outer shell:
cast glass

inner organs / mouthpieces:
soft 3D printed silicone

base medium:
formed mycelium block using appropriate hardwoods as its base (see inoculation requirements)

central cistern:
blown glass

(a) outer shell:
protective and variegated surface containing transpiration pods for companion species

(b) transpiration pods:
pods within the outer shell collect water from transpiration of companion species - plants, mushroom, etc

(c) inner organs:
inner organ layer carries condensed water from vapor towards subgrade cistern following the logic of mycellium hyphae as water transport network

(d) mouthpieces:
mouthpieces extend from the inner organ layer out through the outer shell, extending to collect human breath

(e) base layer:
the base layer exists between the inner organs and the central cistern and supports the shiitake mushroom (and other companion species), allowing water to pass through these organisms, filtering out pollutants before entering the cistern

(f) water grooves:
grooving in the base layer acts as a water channel to aid in the movement of water toward the central cistern

(g) inoculation site:
inner-most area of the base serves as the innnoculation site for the Shiitake (see inoculation stages for details)

(h) central cistern:
all liquid converges into a central cistern that collects the water from our collective and interspecies exhale, passing it though companion species of mushrooms which purify and dehumanize the liquid for greater use within the constructed ecosystem

system **components**

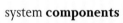

companion **species**

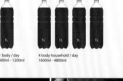

Common Name: Shiitake (from "shii" meaning "from hardwood trees" in Japanese)

Scientific Name: Lentinula edodes

Kingdom: Fungi

Optimum Habitat: Requires shade, moisture, protection from wind, and prefers a warm and isolated environment (i.e., does not compete well with other wild fungi)

Inoculation Requirements: Shiitakes can be inoculated on oak, maple, beech, ironwood, chestnut, sweetgum, poplar, hornbeam, ironwood, mulberry, and chinquapin.

Inoculation Requirements: Holes 3" apart are drilled into the mycelium base, itself made up of the wood specified above. Plugs consisting of fungal inoculum are inserted into the holes and sealed with cheese wax, bees wax or paraffin. The inoculated area should be raised above the ground, and in 80 percent to full shade. Direct sun and wind can damage the early fungal growth or "spawn", and can dry out the base. The fungus needs moisture to grow. Ideally, moisture content should be above 35 percent. After a "spawn run" period, the fungus will "colonize" or grow through the base.

Nutritional Requirements: Shiitake feed on ammonia, carbon, and volitile organic compounds.

Inoculation stages:

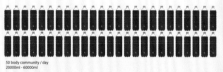

base:
formed mycelium block

holes:
diameter holes 15cm apart

spore pegs:
insert spore pegs in holes

seal:
seal spore in hole with wax

sprout:
feeding on moisture and nutrition from human breath, mushrooms will sprout, filtering the water as it passes through its body and producing surplus water through guttation to contribute to the communal cistern

what is in a **breath?**

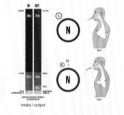
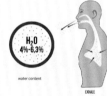

intake / output

water content

EXHALE

The air humans breathe becomes humidified by our aqueous interior before it is exhaled. All breath is a process of exchange. Exhaled air from humans contains approximately 75.0% Nitrogen, 15.0% Oxygen, 0.9% Argon, 4.0% Carbon Dioxide and 5.0%-6.3% water – released fifteen to twenty-five times per minute.

The average human takes in 2500 ml of water per day through foods, beverages and metabolism. The output of water is the same as the input, 2500 ml, of which 29% is considered invisible loss through the mucus membrane and our lungs.

The moisture content in the average human breath (of which there are 23,040 per day), could theoretically produce between 400 ml to 1,200 ml of water per day for one person and up to 60,000 ml per day by a community of 50.

1 body / day
400ml - 1200ml

4 body household / day
1600ml - 4800ml

50 body community / day
20000ml - 60000ml

emergent **processes**

initial companion species:
Shiitake mushroom

HUMAN BREATH

HYDRATION
WATER
AMMONIA/VOC
NUTRITION

FUNGI

Metabolic Water creation

DEHUMANIZE
+ AMPLIFY
WATER

Guttation

The designed system is not meant to create a closed loop but over time will extend to supply water to other organisms that would become the co-inhabitants of this new emergent ecosystem.

emergent companion species:
bryophyta species

Transpiration

PLANT

WATER
CARBON DIOXIDE
HYDRATION

HUMAN
BREATH

WATER
AMMONIA/VOC
NUTRITION

FUNGI

Metabolic Water creation

TRANSPIRATION
WATER
SUGAR

DEHUMANIZE
+ AMPLIFY
WATER

Guttation

The fungus provides two integral elements to fuel and sustain this designed ecosystem. First, as the water from the breath passes though the fungus to enable its growth, the fungus filters the impurities in that liquid – "dehumanizing" the water in the process. Second, the fungus creates surplus water through the metabolism of plant waste – known as metabolic water – which it subsequently exhales or excretes out of its body.

system **logics**

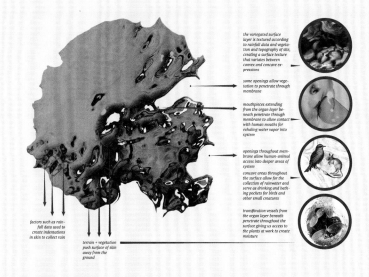

the variegated surface layer is textured according to rainfall data and vegetation and topography of site, creating a surface texture that variates between convex and concave expressions

some openings allow vegetation to penetrate through membrane

mouthpieces extending from the organ layer beneath penetrate through membrane to allow contact with human mouths for exhaling water vapor into system

openings throughout membrane allow human-animal access into deeper areas of system

concave areas throughout the surface allow for the collection of rainwater and serve as drinking and bathing pockets for birds and other small creatures

transpiration vessels from the organ layer beneath penetrate throughout the surface giving us access to the plants at work to create moisture

factors such as rainfall data used to create indentations in skin to collect rain

terrain + vegetation push surface of skin away from the ground

DAN PARKER
STANISLAV ROUDAVSKI

POWERFUL OWL *Ninox strenua*

Growing human impact degrades or eliminates habitats of many lifeforms. In response, this project designs and installs prosthetic habitats for the powerful owl within the ecosystem of greater Melbourne, Australia. The term "prosthetic habitats" refers to a regenerative design strategy, which aims to reinstate absent habitat opportunities by grafting elements onto existing structures. Urbanization and consequent habitat loss threaten the survival of powerful owls. Ongoing development compels owls to enter cities in search of food; however, the hollows in large old trees that owls rely on as breeding habitat are increasingly rare and take hundreds of years to form. To support displaced wildlife, ecologists and conservationists install artificial habitats. But in the case of powerful owls, nest boxes have only once successfully supported breeding and, even then, one of the two chicks died. This project addresses this by using digital form-making and fabrication techniques to design habitats that better suit the needs and preferences of powerful owls.

The project combines the expertise of architects, engineers, biologists, ecologists, city government, park authorities, and arborists. The resulting designs draw inspiration from the natural habitat structures that owls have used for nesting: tree hollows and termite nests. To resemble these habitats, the design process uses algorithmic modelling to account for owl behavior and hollow geometries. The resulting prosthetic nests can adapt to different sites and serve other species, at multiple scales. Augmented reality makes it easy to assemble the nests' complex shapes from 3D-printed wood blocks. The semi-automated workflow makes design accessible to non-experts who can customize designs to suit local needs. On-site monitoring found that prosthetic nests provide better thermal comfort than typical nest boxes. The owl project serves as a demonstration of the possibilities of prosthetic habitats, which can be applied to many species and ecosystems.

Prosthetic Habitats

for the Powerful Owl (Ninox strenua)

Prosthetic Nest precisely fitting a large Eucalyptus tree

Powerful owl chick in a natural tree hollow

Credit: Bradsworth (2015)

Credit: Jackson (2012)

Client

The powerful owl is Australia's largest owl. Sadly, urbanization and consequent habitat loss threaten their survival. The hollows in large old trees that owls rely on for breeding are increasingly rare. Such hollows take some 150-500 years to form. Human-made structures have only once supported breeding of these owls and even then, one of the two chicks died. In response, this project uses digital form-making and fabrication techniques to design habitats that better suit the needs and preferences of owls. The resulting designs draw inspiration from the natural habitat structures that owls have used for nesting: tree hollows and termite nests.

Precedent: Natural Hollow

Accommodates both parents and two young

Shelters from wind, rain, and temperature extremes

Supports nesting for many years

Credit: Blantyre (2009)

Precedent: Termite Nest

Adds nesting sites to young and healthy trees that have no natural hollows

Self-organizes around branches

Regulates temperature and ventilation

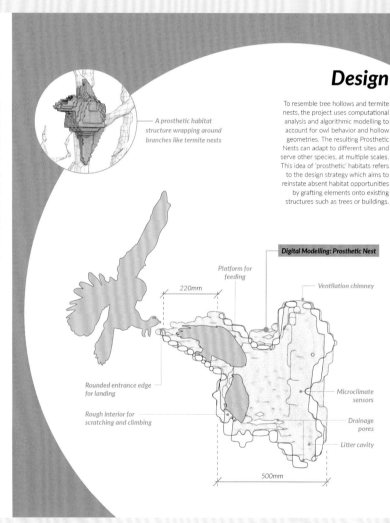

A prosthetic habitat structure wrapping around branches like termite nests

Design

To resemble tree hollows and termite nests, the project uses computational analysis and algorithmic modelling to account for owl behavior and hollow geometries. The resulting Prosthetic Nests can adapt to different sites and serve other species, at multiple scales. This idea of 'prosthetic' habitats refers to the design strategy which aims to reinstate absent habitat opportunities by grafting elements onto existing structures such as trees or buildings.

Digital Modelling: Prosthetic Nest

Platform for feeding

Ventilation chimney

220mm

Rounded entrance edge for landing

Rough interior for scratching and climbing

Microclimate sensors

Drainage pores

Litter cavity

500mm

Engagement

Computational mapping identifies feasible locations for prosthetic additions in human-populated areas by accounting for habitat preferability, tree cover, roosting-tree types, proximity to waterways, roads, buildings, and urban heat islands. After locating the site, 3D scanning of the host-tree helps to position the Prosthetic Nests. These tools provide the basis for solidarity building, collaboration and learning because they embed the expertise of residents, volunteer groups, local managers, arborists, and ecologists. Augmented reality makes it easy to assemble complex shapes from a variety of organic based materials. The semi-automated workflow makes design accessible to non-experts who can customize designs to suit local needs. Monitoring of occupancy provides live data feeds for the engagement with the human public and an online configurator (not shown) supports customization of nests to match the needs of other species.

Siting: Computational Map

Melbourne, Australia

1000m

Best Habitat

Good Habitat

Some Habitat

Site *No Habitat* *Poor Habitat*

Selection of best attachment points

Locating positions at crotch junctions for easy installation

Avoiding areas that are structurally unsound

Limiting the search space to heights where owls usually nest (8-15m)

Finding positions oriented towards the South-East to avoid excessive heat gain

5m

Knotted harness can support all forms of nests

Custom fitting to laser-scanned trees makes installation easy

Coir (natural fibre) provides a soft buffer between the nest and the tree

Weight: 15kg
For comparison, typical nest boxes of this size weigh 25kg and carved hollows are over 250kg

Functional Prototypes: Prosthetic Nests

Option 1: Hempcrete (left)
Option 2: 3D Printed Wood (right)
Both materials are biodegradable, non-toxic, and durable

Wearer's point of view without digital overlay

Construction optimisation algorithm guides the placement of modules that vary in shapes, sizes, porosities, and functions

Augmented reality headsets make assembly easy and accessible

3D printed wood modules (25mm high)

Construction: Augmented Reality Assembly

AASHTI MILLER
AITOR FRÍAS-SÁNCHEZ
JOAQUÍN PERAILES-SANTIAGO

ORB-WEAVER SPIDER *Araneidae*

The Chernobyl Exclusion Zone (CEZ) has become an unexpected refuge for wildlife. This surprising fact is both an inspiring manifestation of the resilience of life, and a sad example of how nuclear radiation, despite its disastrous effects, is less of an obstacle to animals than humans. This proposal focuses specifically on the orb-weaver spiders of the Araneidae family. These creatures have been making erratic and less effective webs as a result of the challenging environment of the CEZ. Moreover, this family of spiders has a high adaptation capacity, which is why we have opted not to replace, but rather augment their web-making processes to improve their chances of survival.

We propose artificially constructing the general framework of their webs, after which the spiders themselves can focus on creating the most important part of the structure: the spiral made of sticky silk, which captures insects. Spiders expend a large amount of energy to create the framework, hence our proposal ensures that they can solely work on the production and weaving of the sticky silk, reacquiring their hunting capabilities over time with minimal human intervention.

We imagine that an aggregate of these webs creates a mobile architectural device, which can contain and transport a healthy cluster of spiders. Various sensors control the "legs," which can select optimum locations and orientations for increased insect capture. The legs will only move for a maximum of two hours a day, and always during the daytime when the spiders are inactive. Their movements will be extremely slow and organic, preventing any disruptive vibrations. Our design seeks to generate a disturbing and calm presence inserted in this post-apocalyptic context. Under the human gaze, these life-bearing artifacts will interact directly with the imaginary subconscious itself.

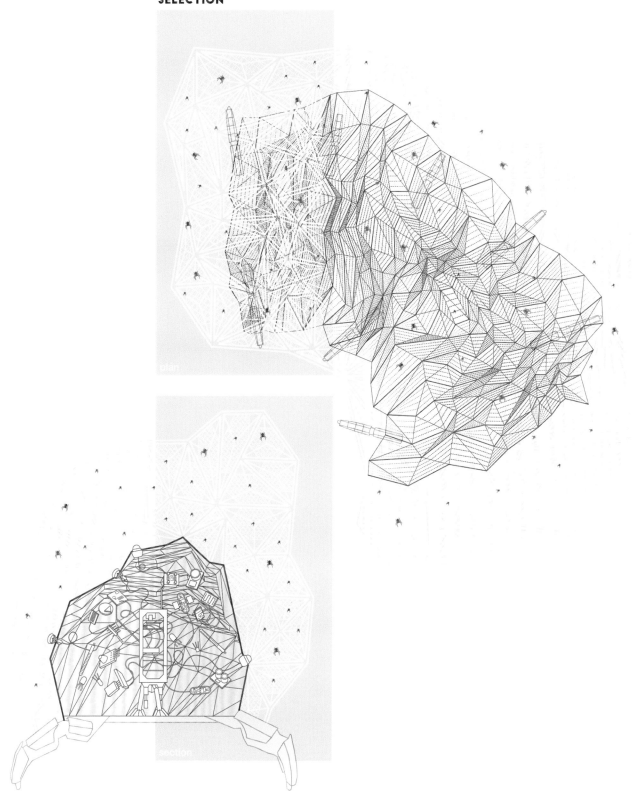

WHY THIS CREATURE?

The Chernobyl Exclusion Zone (CEZ) has become an unexpected refuge for wildlife. This surprising fact is both an inspiring manifestation of the resilience of life & a sad example of how nuclear radiation, despite its disastrous effects, is less of an obstacle to animals than humans.

Specifically, we are focusing on weaver spiders of the "Araneidae" family, which have been making erratic & less effective webs. This is directly affecting their chances of survival.

WHAT ARE THE CRITICAL FEATURES OF THE SPECIES?

- Spiders use their own body for measurements to construct webs in vertical planes
- Spiders improve their web designs based on their hunting experience
- Common nocturnal orb-web spiders are found in clumped dispersion patterns in the vicinity of artificial lights and water
- Araneidae have a high adaptation capacity

chernobyl, ukraine

HOW DO WE FULFILL THEIR NEEDS?

After building the general framework of the web, spiders build the most important part of the web: the spiral made of sticky silk, which captures insects. The spiders expend a large amount of energy to create these structures, so our project proposes artificially reproducing web framework to ensure that spiders can solely focus on the production & weaving of the sticky silk.

artificial spider web

HOW DO WE INCREASE HUMAN AWARENESS TOWARDS THEM?

We imagine a mobile architectural device capable of containing & transporting a healthy cluster of spiders. The design seeks to generate a disturbing & calm presence inserted in this post-apocalyptic context. Under the human gaze, these life-bearing artifacts will interact directly with the imaginary subconscious itself.

HOW DO THEY ENGAGE WITH THEIR ENVIRONMENT?

Various sensors control the "legs", which can select optimum locations and orientations for increased insect capture. The legs will only move for a maximum of two hours a day, and always during the daytime, when the spiders are inactive. Leg movements will be extremely slow and organic preventing any disruptive vibrations.

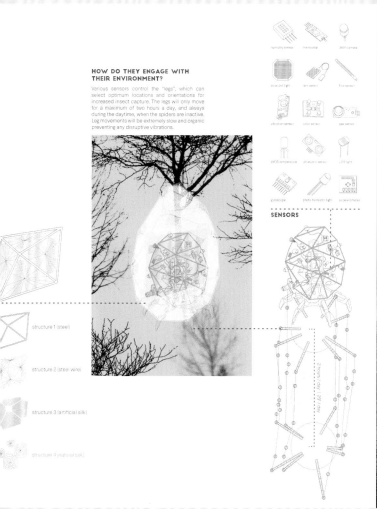

structure 1 (steel)

structure 2 (steel wire)

structure 3 (artificial silk)

structure 4 (natural silk)

SENSORS

CONOR O'SHEA

BROOD XIII 17-YEAR PERIODICAL CICADA *Magicicada septendecim + Magicicada cassini*

November 5, 2020 | CHICAGO | On Wednesday, City Council passed a set of amendments to the Municipal Code known locally as the "Cicada Code." The code will be injected into Chapter 10-32 and Chapter 17-11, thereby amending Chicago's landscape ordinance. Brood XIII of the 17-year periodical cicada *Magicicada spp.* is expected to reemerge in 2024, and these changes will ensure its survival and communicate its importance to the public. They are also intended to be an ecological trojan horse: while benefiting the cicada, they will create bottom-up cascades.

In her closing statement, Mayor Lori E. Lightfoot said, "I would be hard-pressed to find a councilperson who doesn't have fond memories of the 17-year cicadas. We must preserve that memory for future generations and in the process improve our city's resiliency. With the Brood XIII emergence only four years away, the time to act is now."

Aside from the awesome natural spectacle the emergence provides, other benefits cited by the team that helped write the code included pruning mature trees, aerating the soil, and increasing rainwater infiltration through cicadas' emergence holes. As one of nature's great "resource pulses," cicadas provide nitrogen for trees, increase microbial biomass, and feed birds and mammals.

The highlights of the code include the creation of the Chicago Cicada District (CCD), a three-square-mile area in the city's northwest side with special requirements. Other amendments overturn outmoded maintenance practices, like removing leaf litter and spraying insecticides, both now banned in the CCD and in parkways and medians across the city. In addition to placing educational signage in the CCD, the Department of Cultural Affairs and Special Events will host nocturnal visits to cicada emergence sites and listening tours during late summer of 2024 led by acoustical experts from Northeastern Illinois University and the Chicago Symphony Orchestra.

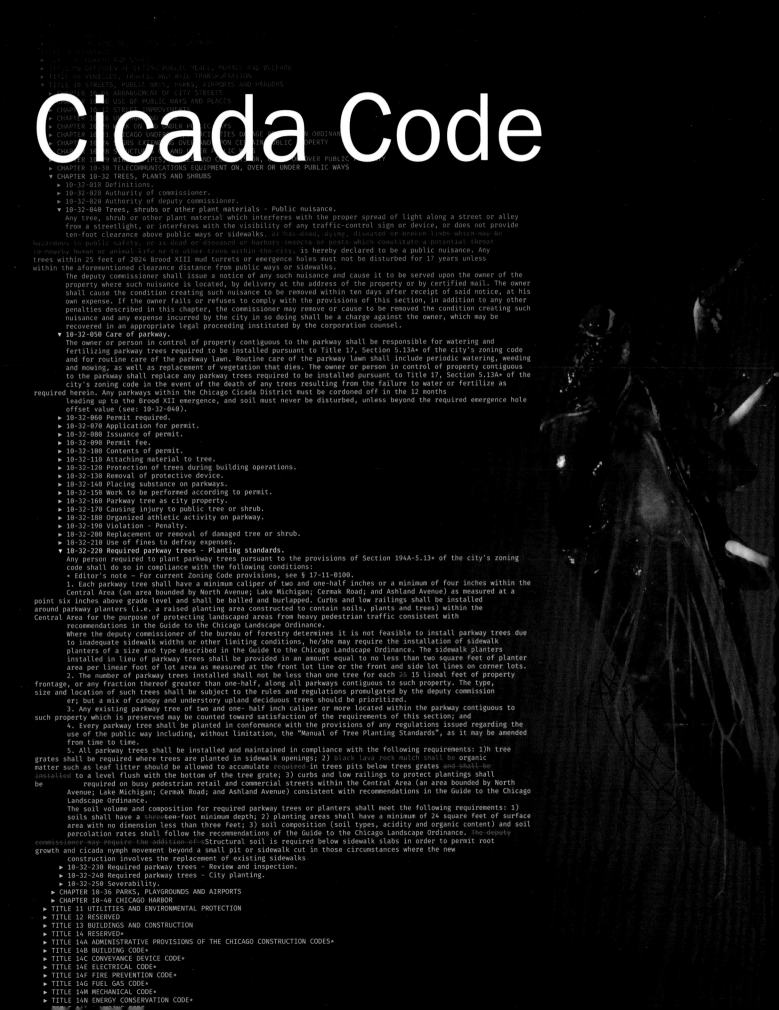

Cicada Code

    ► 10-32-010 Definitions.
    ► 10-32-020 Authority of commissioner.
    ► 10-32-020 Authority of deputy commissioner.
    ▼ 10-32-040 Trees, shrubs or other plant materials - Public nuisance.

Any tree, shrub or other plant material which interferes with the proper spread of light along a street or alley from a streetlight, or interferes with the visibility of any traffic-control sign or device, or does not provide ten-foot clearance above public ways or sidewalks, or has dead, dying, diseased or broken limbs which may be hazardous to public safety, or is dead or diseased or harbors insects or pests which constitute a potential threat to nearby human or animal life or to other trees within the city, is hereby declared to be a public nuisance. Any trees within 25 feet of 2024 Brood XIII mud turrets or emergence holes must not be disturbed for 17 years unless within the aforementioned clearance distance from public ways or sidewalks.

The deputy commissioner shall issue a notice of any such nuisance and cause it to be served upon the owner of the property where such nuisance is located, by delivery at the address of the property or by certified mail. The owner shall cause the condition creating such nuisance to be removed within ten days after receipt of said notice, at his own expense. If the owner fails or refuses to comply with the provisions of this section, in addition to any other penalties described in this chapter, the commissioner may remove or cause to be removed the condition creating such nuisance and any expense incurred by the city in so doing shall be a charge against the owner, which may be recovered in an appropriate legal proceeding instituted by the corporation counsel.

    ▼ 10-32-050 Care of parkway.

The owner or person in control of property contiguous to the parkway shall be responsible for watering and fertilizing parkway trees required to be installed pursuant to Title 17, Section 5.13A* of the city's zoning code and for routine care of the parkway lawn. Routine care of the parkway lawn shall include periodic watering, weeding and mowing, as well as replacement of vegetation that dies. The owner or person in control of property contiguous to the parkway shall replace any parkway trees required to be installed pursuant to Title 17, Section 5.13A* of the city's zoning code in the event of the death of any trees resulting from the failure to water or fertilize as required herein. Any parkways within the Chicago Cicada District must be cordoned off in the 12 months leading up to the Brood XII emergence, and soil must never be disturbed, unless beyond the required emergence hole offset value (see: 10-32-040).

    ► 10-32-060 Permit required.
    ► 10-32-070 Application for permit.
    ► 10-32-080 Issuance of permit.
    ► 10-32-090 Permit fee.
    ► 10-32-100 Contents of permit.
    ► 10-32-110 Attaching material to tree.
    ► 10-32-120 Protection of trees during building operations.
    ► 10-32-130 Removal of protective device.
    ► 10-32-140 Placing substance on parkways.
    ► 10-32-150 Work to be performed according to permit.
    ► 10-32-160 Parkway tree as city property.
    ► 10-32-170 Causing injury to public tree or shrub.
    ► 10-32-180 Organized athletic activity on parkway.
    ► 10-32-190 Violation - Penalty.
    ► 10-32-200 Replacement or removal of damaged tree or shrub.
    ► 10-32-210 Use of fines to defray expenses.
    ▼ 10-32-220 Required parkway trees - Planting standards.

Any person required to plant parkway trees pursuant to the provisions of Section 194A-5.13* of the city's zoning code shall do so in compliance with the following conditions:

* Editor's note – For current Zoning Code provisions, see § 17-11-0100.

1. Each parkway tree shall have a minimum caliper of two and one-half inches or a minimum of four inches within the Central Area (an area bounded by North Avenue; Lake Michigan; Cermak Road; and Ashland Avenue) as measured at a point six inches above grade level and shall be balled and burlapped. Curbs and low railings shall be installed around parkway planters (i.e. a raised planting area constructed to contain soils, plants and trees) within the Central Area for the purpose of protecting landscaped areas from heavy pedestrian traffic consistent with recommendations in the Guide to the Chicago Landscape Ordinance.

Where the deputy commissioner of the bureau of forestry determines it is not feasible to install parkway trees due to inadequate sidewalk widths or other limiting conditions, he/she may require the installation of sidewalk planters of a size and type described in the Guide to the Chicago Landscape Ordinance. The sidewalk planters installed in lieu of parkway trees shall be provided in an amount equal to no less than two square feet of planter area per linear foot of lot area as measured at the front lot line or the front and side lot lines on corner lots.

2. The number of parkway trees installed shall not be less than one tree for each 25 15 lineal feet of property frontage, or any fraction thereof greater than one-half, along all parkways contiguous to such property. The type, size and location of such trees shall be subject to the rules and regulations promulgated by the deputy commissioner; but a mix of canopy and understory upland deciduous trees should be prioritized.

3. Any existing parkway tree of two and one- half inch caliper or more located within the parkway contiguous to such property which is preserved may be counted toward satisfaction of the requirements of this section; and

4. Every parkway tree shall be planted in conformance with the provisions of any regulations issued regarding the use of the public way including, without limitation, the "Manual of Tree Planting Standards", as it may be amended from time to time.

5. All parkway trees shall be installed and maintained in compliance with the following requirements: 1)h tree grates shall be required where trees are planted in sidewalk openings; 2) black lava rock mulch shall be organic matter such as leaf litter should be allowed to accumulate required in trees pits below trees grates and shall be installed to a level flush with the bottom of the tree grate; 3) curbs and low railings to protect plantings shall be required on busy pedestrian retail and commercial streets within the Central Area (an area bounded by North Avenue; Lake Michigan; Cermak Road; and Ashland Avenue) consistent with recommendations in the Guide to the Chicago Landscape Ordinance.

The soil volume and composition for required parkway trees or planters shall meet the following requirements: 1) soils shall have a three ten-foot minimum depth; 2) planting areas shall have a minimum of 24 square feet of surface area with no dimension less than three feet; 3) soil composition (soil types, acidity and organic content) and soil percolation rates shall follow the recommendations of the Guide to the Chicago Landscape Ordinance. The deputy commissioner may require the addition of sStructural soil is required below sidewalk slabs in order to permit root growth and cicada nymph movement beyond a small pit or sidewalk cut in those circumstances where the new construction involves the replacement of existing sidewalks.

    ► 10-32-230 Required parkway trees - Review and inspection.
    ► 10-32-240 Required parkway trees - City planting.
    ► 10-32-250 Severability.

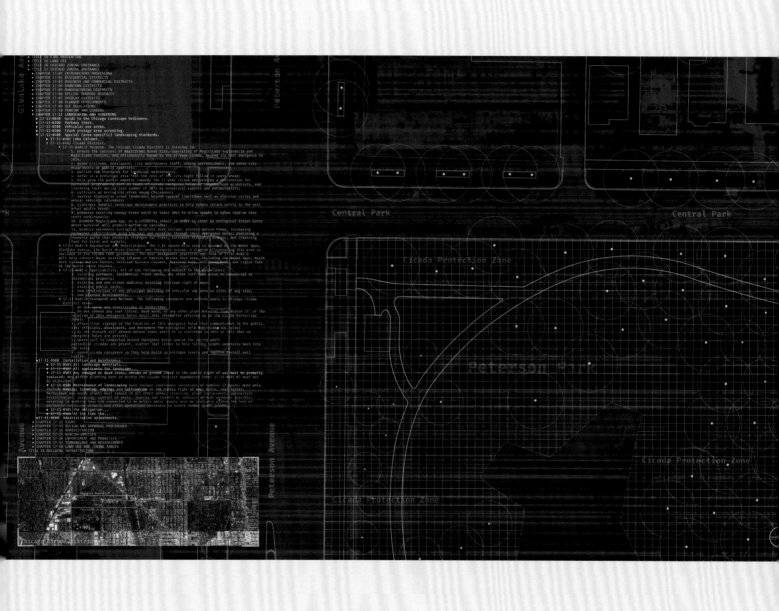

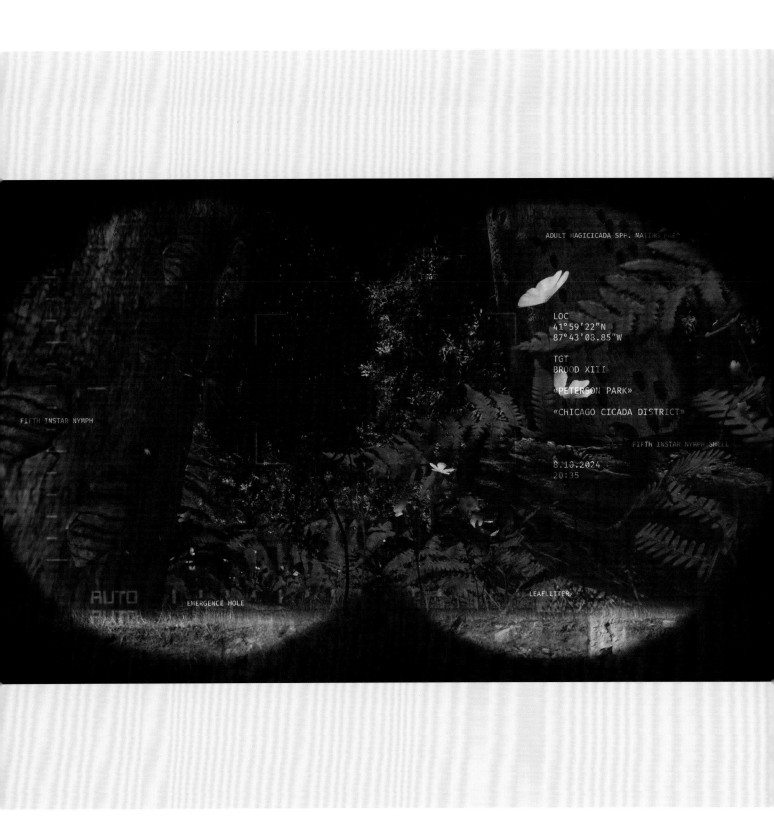

HUONG DINH

NORTHERN LEOPARD FROG *Lithobates pipiens*

The northern leopard frog is familiar to most people as the frog they dissect in their middle school biology class. Challenging this mode of presenting animals as still, isolated objects in school labs, "Life of L" is a curriculum that proposes an alternative approach to learning about animals. In this classroom, students are invited to take a journey through the unfamiliar world of frogs to understand them as lively, animate subjects: they no longer appear as *Lithobates pipiens* but as L – the protagonist in their own story with their unique worldview, or umwelt, to use Jakob von Uexküll's term.

The curriculum is thus a cartographic project that attempts to chart this curious world of L, using maps both as a structure for the class and as a notational method. As such, it proposes a general scheme that can be adapted to various locations where L's habitats can be discovered and engaged. Each of the six chapters of the journey aims to directly enhance L's life by guiding children to aid L's various needs – namely food, migration, reproduction, and shelter. The proposed activities are designed for participants of all skill levels to carry out using everyday materials, yet they also demand a tremendous amount of patience and respect in order to see the elusive L and to understand both their similarities and differences from us, including the body's vulnerability to infectious diseases and the surrounding environment. Ultimately, the project seeks to benefit L by setting up a catalytic framework for their relationships with youth—the next generation of scientists, conservationists, park rangers, and road builders—who can work together to address the global threats facing both L and humans alike.

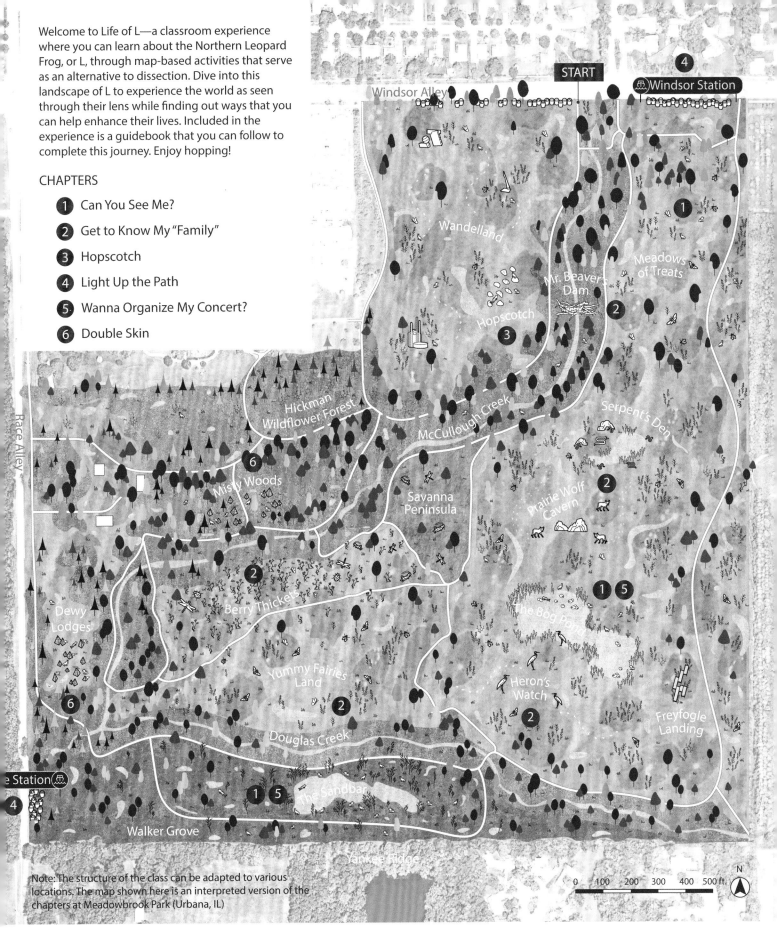

Welcome to Life of L—a classroom experience where you can learn about the Northern Leopard Frog, or L, through map-based activities that serve as an alternative to dissection. Dive into this landscape of L to experience the world as seen through their lens while finding out ways that you can help enhance their lives. Included in the experience is a guidebook that you can follow to complete this journey. Enjoy hopping!

CHAPTERS

1. Can You See Me?
2. Get to Know My "Family"
3. Hopscotch
4. Light Up the Path
5. Wanna Organize My Concert?
6. Double Skin

Note: The structure of the class can be adapted to various locations. The map shown here is an interpreted version of the chapters at Meadowbrook Park (Urbana, IL)

0 100 200 300 400 500 ft.

N

LIFE OF L

An Alternative Curriculum to Classroom Dissection

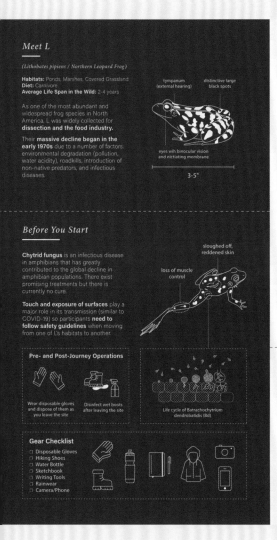

Meet L

(Lithobates pipiens / Northern Leopard Frog)

Habitats: Ponds, Marshes, Covered Grassland
Diet: Carnivore
Average Life Span in the Wild: 2-4 years

As one of the most abundant and widespread frog species in North America, L was widely collected for **dissection and the food industry.**

Their **massive decline began in the early 1970s** due to a number of factors: environmental degradation (pollution, water acidity), roadkills, introduction of non-native predators, and infectious diseases.

Before You Start

Chytrid fungus is an infectious disease in amphibians that has greatly contributed to the global decline in amphibian populations. There exist promising treatments but there is currently no cure.

Touch and exposure of surfaces play a major role in its transmission (similar to COVID-19) so participants **need to follow safety guidelines** when moving from one of L's habitats to another.

Pre- and Post-Journey Operations

Wear disposable gloves and dispose of them as you leave the site

Disinfect wet boots after leaving the site

Life cycle of Batrachochytrium dendrobatidis (Bd)

Gear Checklist
☐ Disposable Gloves
☐ Hiking Shoes
☐ Water Bottle
☐ Sketchbook
☐ Writing Tools
☐ Rainwear
☐ Camera/Phone

Chapter 1. Can You See Me?

Visual perception is one of the first ways in which humans are familiarized with L. Yet, knowing what they look like is different from **seeing them—registering their presence as lively creatures in their natural habitats.** This first chapter thus asks students to actively find ways to see L, both directly, and indirectly through their **traces or marks—a fundamental form of communication** that extends beyond verbal language.

Learning Questions:

• What does L look like? What are their most distinctive characteristics to you?
• What are their common habitats? Where do they often frequent?

Tasks:

1. Spot L along your path and especially in the areas featuring L in the map
2. Document the spots where you encounter L on the map and mark it in the landscape with the given marker
3. If you don't encounter L, set up a **mud trap** for tracking their marks!

How does this exercise help L?

The markers help highlight L's habitats and the places that they frequent so that visitors can be reminded to not damage these areas.

Chapter 2. Get to Know My "Family"

L's "family" refers to the larger **"biological family"**—the food chain that L and their predators/preys are part of.

Learning Questions:

• Which animals are the predators and preys of L?
• What are the mechanisms that L uses to catch their preys and hide from their predators?

Tasks:

1. Observe what L eats and which animals prey on L
2. Draw a family tree with the obse[rved] members
3. Plant a seed where you observe[d] interactions between the "member[s]"

How does this exercise help L?

New plantings can help attract ins[ects] which make up most of L's diet!

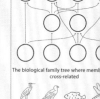

The biological family tree where memb[ers are] cross-related

Heron   Hawk   Fish   Drag[onfly]

Potential members of the family

Chapter 3. Hopscotch

L was often used for classroom dissection not only because they were abundant but also because their bodies share many similarities with us. Yet, they also possess adaptations that allow them to survive in certain habitats. This chapter thus focuses on the locomotion of L—how their body develops to allow for distinct movement patterns.

Learning Questions:

• What are the different movements / actions that L can take?
• How does L's anatomy aid these movements / actions?

Tasks:

1. Hold a photo contest to see who gets the best shots of L's poses
2. Note which body parts aid with the movements/actions that you have recorded or why L holds certain poses
3. Measure how far L jumps and create a hopscotch based on that measurement and their movement pattern
4. Compare your jump with L's and invite them to join the game

Chapter 4. Light Up the Path

winter, L migrates to deeper lakes to
nate in the mud and later in spring, they
again to ponds for mating. Rainy nights
eir preferred time for the move, yet
ed visibility and slippery road conditions
caused countless roadkills each year.

ning Questions:

at are the migration paths of L?
w can we help them avoid car traffic and
te safely? (other than the method in this

Task:

Operate a safe "ferry service" for L by
following the illustrated steps below.

How does this exercise help L?

The "ferry service" helps L navigate roadway
traffic safely to continue their migration
journey.

soft fence material
so L won't get hurt :)

Passenger aboard!

p drift fences along roads | Line buckets along roads to catch passengers

barrier fences with foil and use them to reflect light onto roads.
t pathway helps guide ferry operators while informing drivers to slow down.

Chapter 5. Wanna Organize My Concert?

L is famous for their sounds—a sweet love
song from the male L to their female
counterparts. To make it even more
romantic, they tend to **sing exclusively
during nighttime at spring onset.**

Learning Questions:

• What sounds does L make?
• How do we compare their sounds with ours?

Parabolic Microphone

Find a suitable parabolic dish (salad bowl,
wok lids, used umbrellas)

Find the focal point: point a laser beam to the
dish and mark where it meets the central shaft

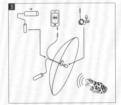

Attach parts to the parabolic dish:

• Arm: Old paint roller with cover removed
• Clip-on microphone

Then connect to an amplifier or recorder. Et
voilà! You are now ready to record L.

Tasks:

To hold a concert and release an album for L:
• Pre-concert: record the "album" with a
parabolic microphone. Separate the album
into daytime and nighttime sections.
• On concert day: Set up **sound visualizers**
near their habitats to create accompanying
visual effects for their concert. You might have
to try different ways to convince L to "take the
mic."

How does this exercise help L?

The "mic" helps amplify L's calls for mates
while lights from the visualizers can attract
moths and insects—a feast for the "singers"
after their concert!

Sound Visualizer

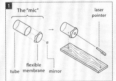

Attach "mic" and lights to stage board. Adjust
pointer so that it points at mirror.

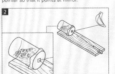

As sounds travel to the "mic", the membrane
and the mirror move, prompting the laser
beam reflection to morph accordingly.

Chapter 6. Double Skin

Skin is one of the most important, yet often
overlooked, organs in the body as it serves
as the first **protective layer** against harmful
external elements. For L, the skin is even
more significant due to its respiratory
function. It is the **semipermeability**
allowing for this function that renders L **far
more sensitive to the surrounding
environment than humans.**

Learning Questions:

• What are the characteristics of L's skin?
• How do the skin's features aid with its
functions?
• How can we address the harmful
environmental factors that affect their skin?

Tasks:

• Build a dew collector (instructions below) to
create a second "skin" for L and invite them to
"wear" it.
• Bonus: Can you upgrade this skin to emulate
more functions of L's skin (eg:
thermoregulation, camouflage)?

How does this exercise help L?

The second "skin" provides still water that can
serve as a **habitat** for L. The openings that are
scaled to only fit L prevent predators from
entering, thus simultaneously turning the
"skin" into a **hideout.**

Build frame for "skin patches"

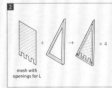

Create "skin patches" by attaching fine mesh to frame

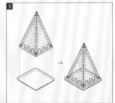

Add tray underneath to collect water

Add treats or other attractions to invite L

Ferry Service | Hopscotch | Misty Woods / Dewy Lodges | The Sandbar | Meadow of Treats

SADIE IMAE
NATALYA DIKHANOV

DESERT RAIN FROG *Breviceps macrops*

The desert rain frog went viral when a 30-second clip of the small, soft, globular, sand-encrusted being appeared on YouTube, squeaking loudly. But this brief stint in the public eye didn't bring attention to its precarious living situation in the delicate coastal ecosystem of South Africa and Namibia, damaged by diamond-mining operations that destroy dunes and displace the endemic flora and fauna that have adapted to live there. As the frog doesn't travel far on its stubby limbs, it can't easily relocate to another suitable habitat. Today, the mining operations have mostly moved on, but not without leaving deep tracks. Additional threats now include transportation, tourism, housing developments, and crop farming.

We propose a transportable pavilion system that plugs into abandoned mining sites to heal the landscape. Mining operations produce acid that leaches into water and soil. Sulfate-reducing bacteria, by feeding on algae, are able to break down harsh metals in the water and return it to normal pH-levels. The polluted water circulates until purified. Once treated, the algae pavilions and bioreactors are moved to the next mining site, and the now-treated water goes to neighboring human communities.

We want to inspire awe of algae, fog, dunes, and the desert rain frog. These phenomena are often considered nuisances, or simply go unnoticed. Here they are openly displayed and celebrated. Nonhumans are the artists of the pavilions' facades – the rising and falling algae levels and condensation generate the texture and decoration of both interior and exterior. Humans, limited to an elevated walkway, can traverse the landscape or walk along the polluted/purifying body of water inside the pavilions. Wooden posts create a field: easy to navigate for frogs, hard for humans. This matrix makes clear that humans are visitors, allowing the dunes to regenerate undisturbed, and restoring home and habitat for the desert rain frog.

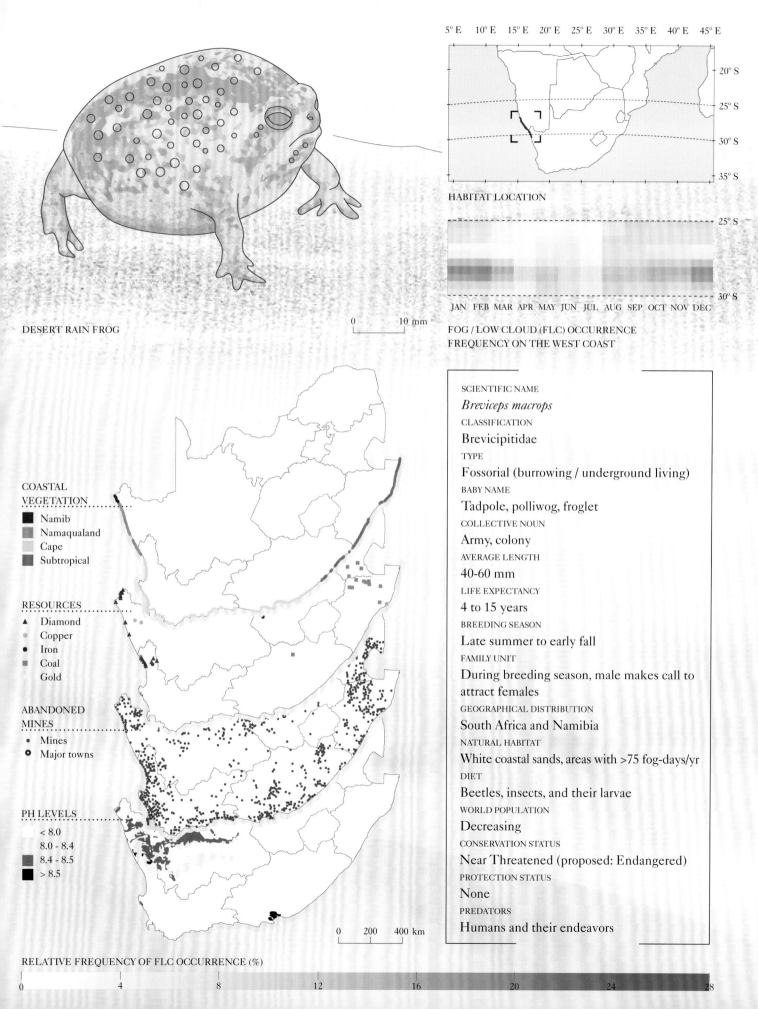

DESERT RAIN FROG

0   10 mm

HABITAT LOCATION

FOG / LOW CLOUD (FLC) OCCURRENCE
FREQUENCY ON THE WEST COAST

JAN FEB MAR APR MAY JUN JUL AUG SEP OCT NOV DEC

COASTAL
VEGETATION
- Namib
- Namaqualand
- Cape
- Subtropical

RESOURCES
- ▲ Diamond
- Copper
- ● Iron
- ■ Coal
- Gold

ABANDONED
MINES
- • Mines
- ○ Major towns

PH LEVELS
- < 8.0
- 8.0 - 8.4
- 8.4 - 8.5
- > 8.5

0   200   400 km

SCIENTIFIC NAME
Breviceps macrops
CLASSIFICATION
Brevicipitidae
TYPE
Fossorial (burrowing / underground living)
BABY NAME
Tadpole, polliwog, froglet
COLLECTIVE NOUN
Army, colony
AVERAGE LENGTH
40-60 mm
LIFE EXPECTANCY
4 to 15 years
BREEDING SEASON
Late summer to early fall
FAMILY UNIT
During breeding season, male makes call to
attract females
GEOGRAPHICAL DISTRIBUTION
South Africa and Namibia
NATURAL HABITAT
White coastal sands, areas with >75 fog-days/yr
DIET
Beetles, insects, and their larvae
WORLD POPULATION
Decreasing
CONSERVATION STATUS
Near Threatened (proposed: Endangered)
PROTECTION STATUS
None
PREDATORS
Humans and their endeavors

RELATIVE FREQUENCY OF FLC OCCURRENCE (%)

0   4   8   12   16   20   24   28

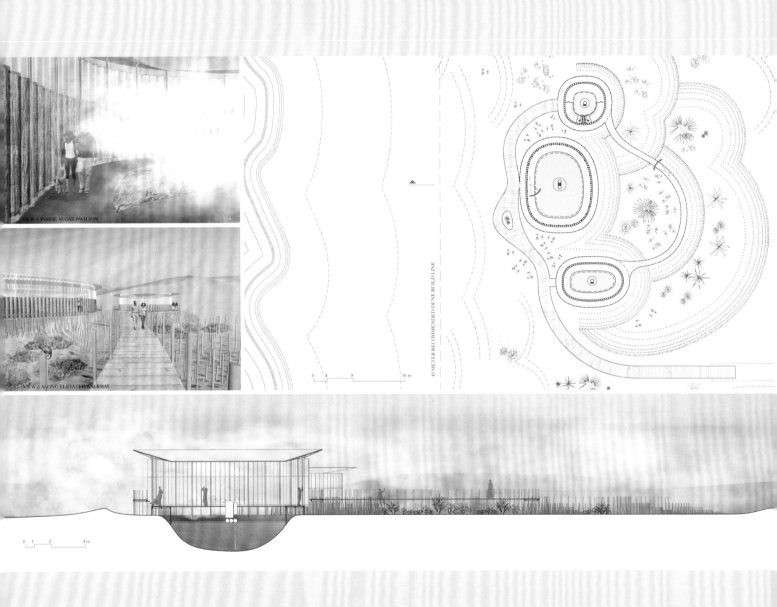

VIEW 1: INSIDE ALGAE PAVILION

VIEW 2: ALONG ELEVATED WALKWAY

45 METER RECOMMENDED DUNE BUILD LINE

0   4   8   16 m

0 1   2   4 m

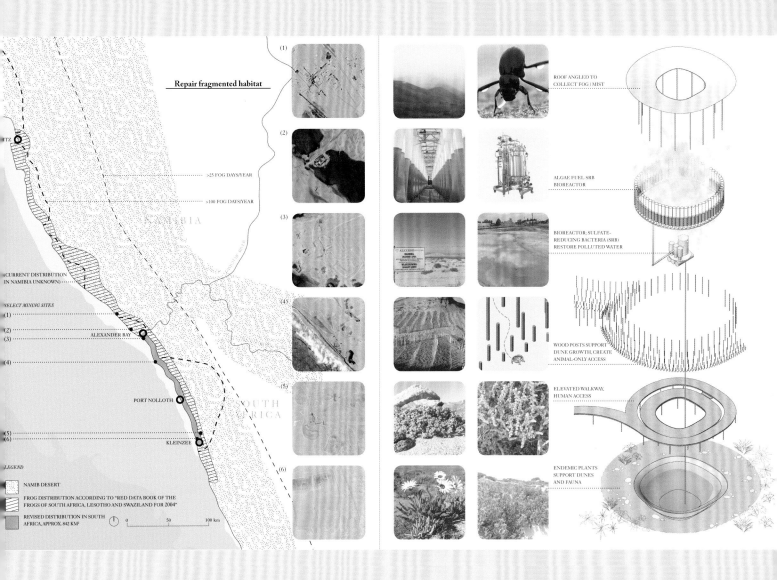

Repair fragmented habitat

>25 FOG DAYS/YEAR

>100 FOG DAYS/YEAR

NAMIBIA

(CURRENT DISTRIBUTION
IN NAMIBIA UNKNOWN)

SELECT MINING SITES

(1)
(2)
(3) ALEXANDER BAY
(4)

PORT NOLLOTH

SOUTH
AFRICA

(5)
(6) KLEINZEE

LEGEND

NAMIB DESERT

FROG DISTRIBUTION ACCORDING TO "RED DATA BOOK OF THE
FROGS OF SOUTH AFRICA, LESOTHO AND SWAZILAND FOR 2004"

REVISED DISTRIBUTION IN SOUTH
AFRICA, APPROX. 842 KM²   0   50   100 km

(1)
(2)
(3)
(4)
(5)
(6)

ROOF ANGLED TO
COLLECT FOG / MIST

ALGAE FUEL SRB
BIOREACTOR

BIOREACTOR; SULFATE-
REDUCING BACTERIA (SRB)
RESTORE POLLUTED WATER

WOOD POSTS SUPPORT
DUNE GROWTH, CREATE
ANIMAL-ONLY ACCESS

ELEVATED WALKWAY,
HUMAN ACCESS

ENDEMIC PLANTS
SUPPORT DUNES
AND FAUNA

YUN WANG
YIRU WANG

CORAL *Anthozoa*

Coral, a sessile animal, forms the basis of the most diverse underwater habitats on Earth. Threatened by the rising temperature and acidity resulting from climate change, coral reefs are being bleached and dying at an alarming rate. The "Coral Cemetery" is a poetic and practical way of bringing much-needed scientific research and public attention to bear on this problem.

The idea is this: cities are running out of space for land burial, so we propose to redirect burial to the ocean floor in areas where coral migration is required. Human remains—sharing a similar chemical composition to coral—along with recycled materials, are collected and processed into modules that sequester carbon and form stable substrate ideal for young coral polyps to colonize. Customers selecting this form of burial will pay a premium to help fund research regarding coral migration as a way of offsetting the debt they have accrued to the environment during their lives.

The cemetery will be a place of remembrance, restoration, and research. Commemoration of the lives, restoration of the stressed coral habitats, and research to pursue a greater understanding of coral and marine ecosystems in an age of rapid climate change.

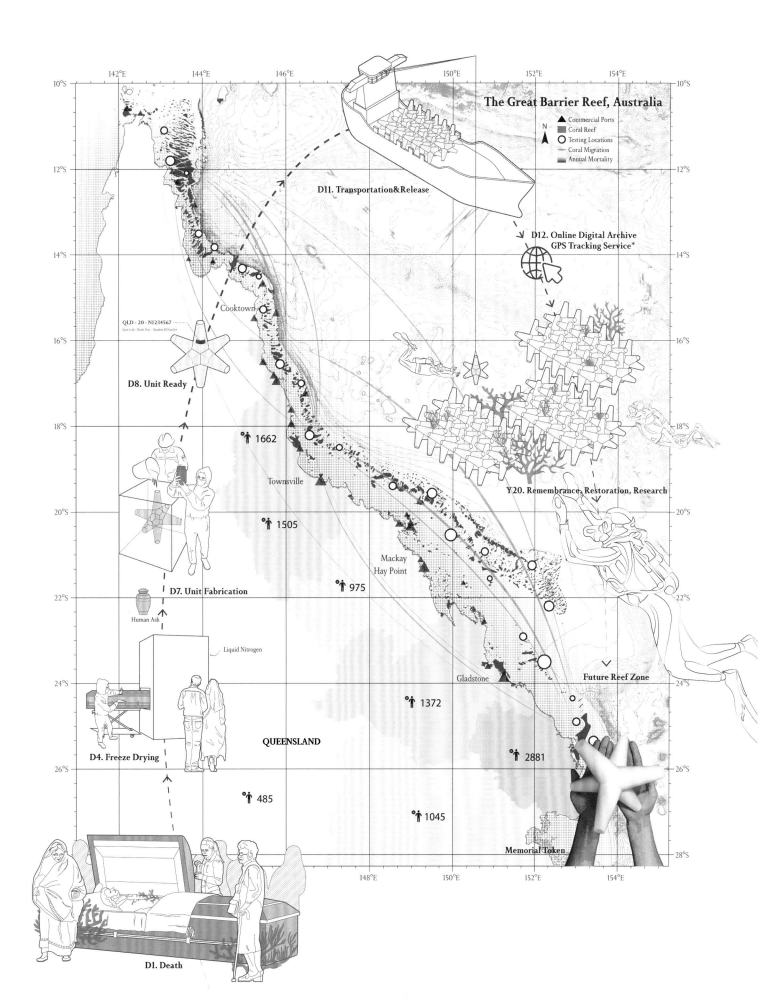

The Great Barrier Reef, Australia

Commercial Ports
Coral Reef
Testing Locations
Coral Migration
Annual Mortality

D11. Transportation&Release

D12. Online Digital Archive
GPS Tracking Service*

Cooktown

QLD - 20 - N1234567
State Code - Death Year - Bracelet ID Number

D8. Unit Ready

D7. Unit Fabrication

Human Ash

Liquid Nitrogen

D4. Freeze Drying

QUEENSLAND

Townsville

Mackay
Hay Point

Gladstone

Y20. Remembrance, Restoration, Research

Future Reef Zone

Memorial Token

D1. Death

1662
1505
975
1372
2881
485
1045

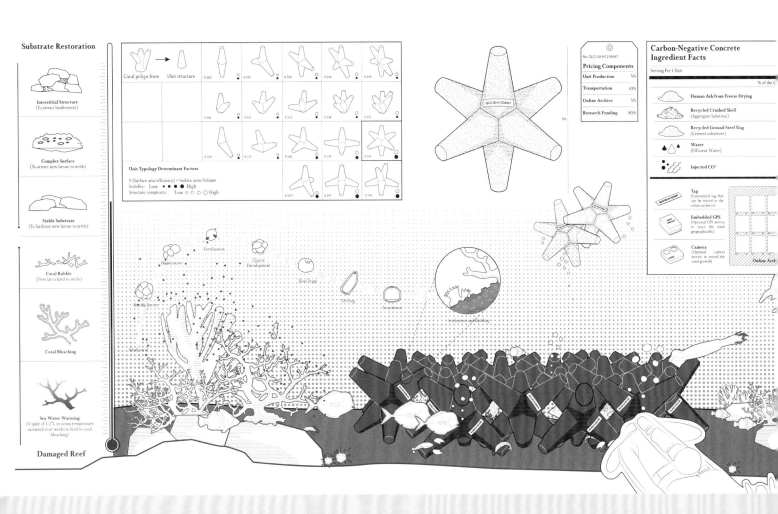

Substrate Restoration

Interstitial Structure
(To attract biodiversity)

Complex Surface
(To attract new larvae to settle)

Stable Substrate
(To facilitate new larvae to settle)

Coral Rubble
(New larva hard to settle)

Coral Bleaching

Sea Water Warming
(A spike of 1-2°C in ocean temperature
sustained over weeks to lead to coral
bleaching)

Damaged Reef

Coral polyps form → Unit structure

Unit Typology Determinant Factors
(Surface area efficiency) = Surface area/Volume
Stability: Low ● ● ● High
Structure complexity: Low ○ ○ ○ ○ High

No. QLD-20-N1234567

Pricing Components

Unit Production	5%
Transportation	10%
Online Archive	5%
Research Funding	80%

Carbon-Negative Concrete Ingredient Facts

Serving Per 1 Unit

% of the C

Human Ash from Freeze Drying

Recycled Crushed Shell
(Aggregate Substitute)

Recycled Ground Steel Slag
(Cement substitute)

Water
(Efficient Water)

Injected CO2

Tag
(Customized tag that
can be traced in the
online archive)

Embedded GPS
(Optional GPS service
to trace the tomb
geographically)

Camera
(Optional camera
service to record the
coral growth)

Online Arch

Humans emitted **43.1 billion tons** of carbon dioxide in 2019.

By 2050, if no action is taken, more than **90%** of the reefs will die.

The projected death number in 2050 is **92.74 million**.

If all use land burial, it requires 146 mi² graveyard space.

If 20% of the population participates in the Coral Cemetery project,

we can create **3 mi²** coral habitats,

sequester **11600 tons** of carbon dioxide annually.

SALON DES

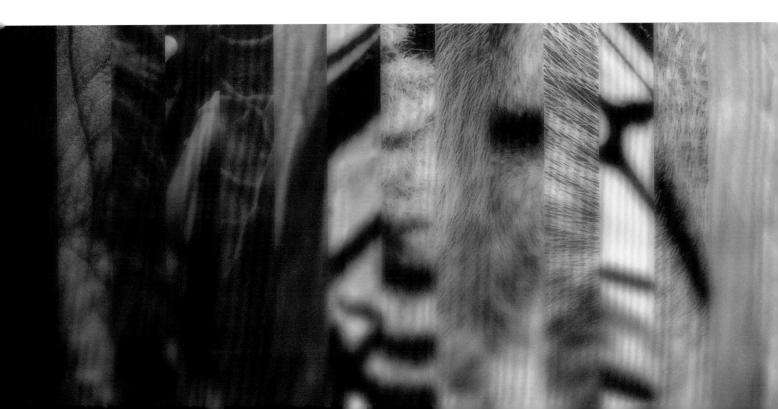

REFUSÉS

Rania Ghosn, El Hadi Jazairy + Anhong Li: A bovine freedom tower comprised of the various typologies used in concentrated animal feeding operations.

It's cozy at the Top
a Great Rock for new ecologies

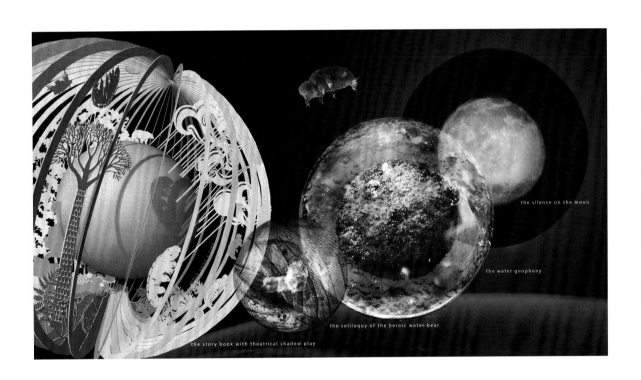

the silence on the moon

the water geophony

the soliloquy of the heroic water bear

the story book with theatrical shadow play

2

1 Thijs de Zeeuw + Bart de Hartog: A massive faux rock rises out of a zoo in Amsterdam to be colonized by multiple, unpredictable species.

2 Goh Yu Han, Wong Mee Na + Yazid Ninsalam: A fiction of how tardigrades (water bears) return to Earth and live in a telescope after a failed space mission to the moon.

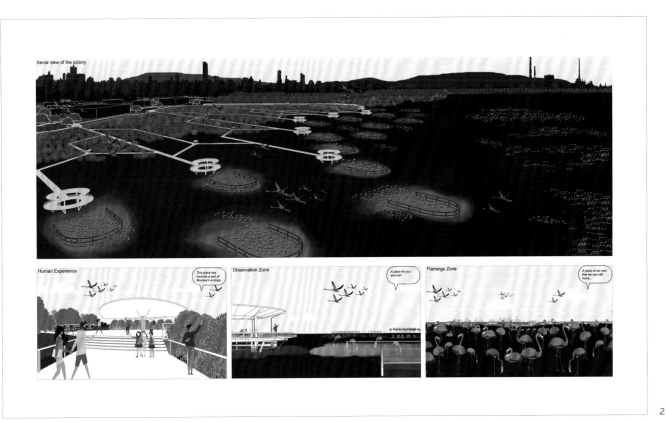

1 Matthew Tucker: A global network of sites ("extinction reliquaries") function in a similar way to UNESCO World Heritage sites by marking places where the last of particular species are known to have lived.

2 Tapasya Mukkamala + Kavya Kalyan: A system for integrating algae production, mangrove restoration, and flamingo habitat in sewerage outfall lagoons in Mumbai.

DOWNSVIEW
ROAMING

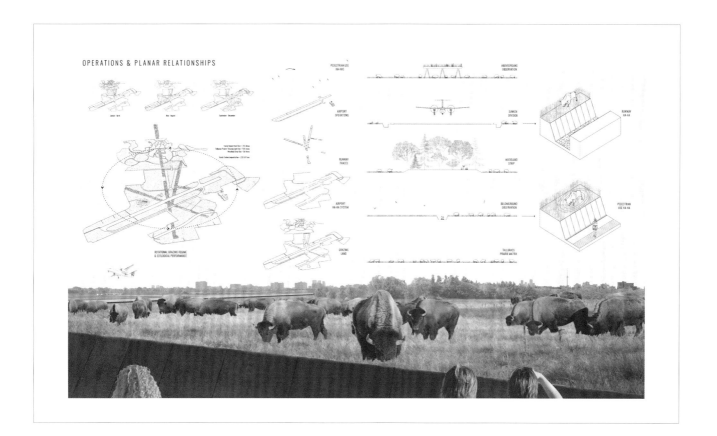

Andrew Taylor: Downsview Park in Toronto is here used as a buffalo sanctuary and incubator and the old airport utilized to distribute the species into rewilding projects across the United States.

American Incarceration

There are 2.3 million people incarcerated in America.

Of the 500,000 individuals released, 2/3 are re-arrested within 2 years.

Correctional Facility Types

U.S. State and Federal Prison Population

U.S. incarceration rates by race and ethnicity 2010

Correctional Facilities Oahu

Currently, 1.5 million children have a parent in prison.

3/4 of individuals released from prison have a history of substance abuse.

Hawaiian Monk Seal

Threats:
Food Limitation
Shark Predation
Entanglement
Habitat loss

Fishery Interactions
Disease
Human-Seal Interactions
Intentional Killing
Male Seal Aggression

Weight 400-600lbs
Lifespan: 30+ years
Length 6-7ft

Diet: Common Fishes, Squid, Eels and Crustaceans

North West Hawaiian Islands

Hawaiian Monk Seal Population (Female)

Life After Prison

Under the Anti-Drug Abuse Act of 1988 and the "One Strike and You're Out" policy adopted by HUD in 1996, people with criminal records are barred from public and subsidized housing. In some cases, local housing authorities have acted to evict family members sheltering relatives with criminal records.

Between 60 to 75 percent of former inmates find themselves jobless up to one year after being released.

It's a very vulnerable space to be in because even when people attempt to hire you, there is prejudice that comes with your past that you can't seem to escape.

Shaka Senghor

Jobs Former Inmates are Barred From:
Firefighter, turnpike employee, bartender, school bus driver, crossing guard, corrections worker, cosmetician, barber. Work Places: nursing homes, airport security, banks, and racetracks.

Unfortunately, when people are sentenced, that sentence never ends — even when they step out of prison.

Many individuals are doing what they can. But real success can only come if there is a change in our societies and in our economics and in our politics.

It seems to me that the natural world is the greatest source of excitement; the greatest source of visual beauty; the greatest source of intellectual interest. It is the greatest source of so much in life that makes life worth living.

David Attenborough

Conservation

Number of Animal Species of the IUCN Red List

Sources of Marine Litter

Endangered Species in Hawaii

Oahu Tree Snail · Green Sea Turtle · Nene Goose · Hawaiian Hoary Bat · Crested Honey creeper · Hawaiian Hawk

1 Bjørn Mündner + Noël Schardt: A million small bird sculptures containing native plant seeds are suspended over Melbourne's Federation Square, where they germinate and are then auctioned to individuals to disperse.

2 Shiori Green: A proposal to link activities necessary to the conservation of the Hawaiian monk seal population to employment programs for people recently released from prison.

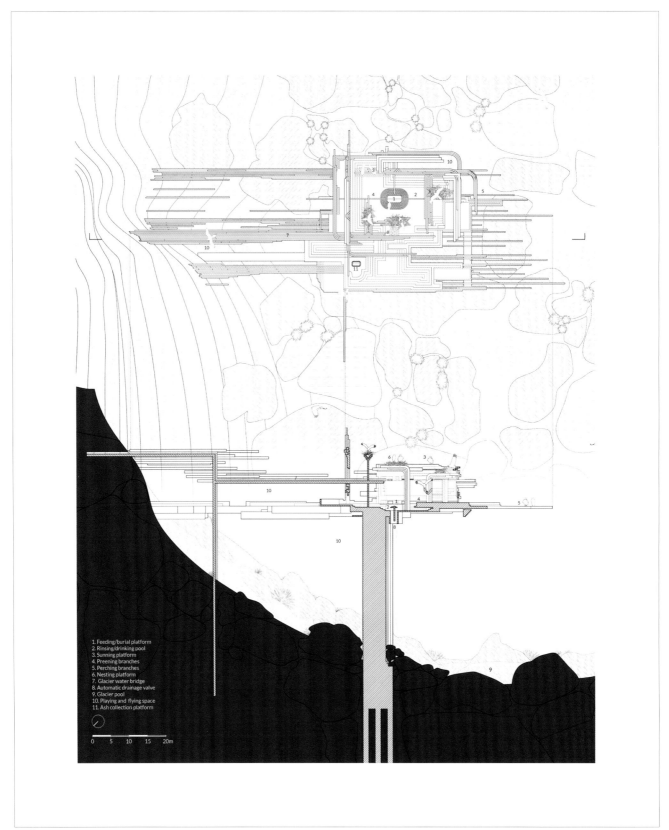

1. Feeding/burial platform
2. Rinsing/drinking pool
3. Sunning platform
4. Preening branches
5. Perching branches
6. Nesting platform
7. Glacier water bridge
8. Automatic drainage valve
9. Glacier pool
10. Playing and flying space
11. Ash collection platform

0   5   10   15   20m

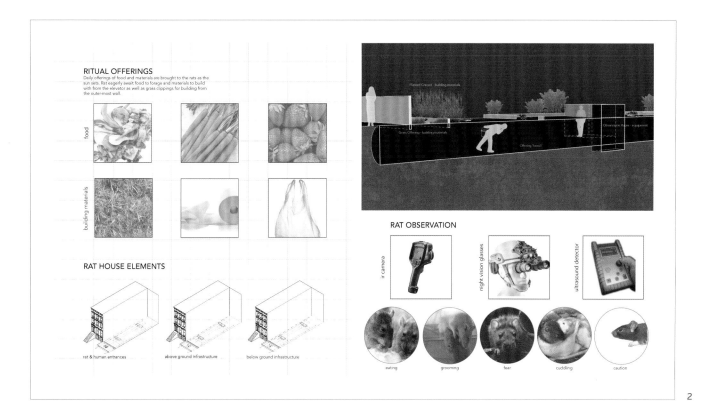

RITUAL OFFERINGS

Daily offerings of food and materials are brought to the rats as the sun sets. Rat eagerly await food to forage and materials to build with from the elevator as well as grass clippings for building from the outer-most wall.

food

building materials

Planted Grassol - building materials

Grass Offering - building materials

Offering Tunnel

Observation Room - equipment

RAT OBSERVATION

ir camera

night vision glasses

ultrasound detector

eating

grooming

fear

cuddling

caution

RAT HOUSE ELEMENTS

rat & human entrances

above ground infrastructure

below ground infrastructure

1 Yushen Jia + Thomas Wang: A structure to offer nesting spaces and also facilitate Tibetan sky burial ceremonies where the deceased are laid out for consumption by vultures.

2 Dana Hills + Tom Wright: The rat house is a safehouse for rats designed to allow humans to enter a dark space and use technology to tune into and see the rats that live there.

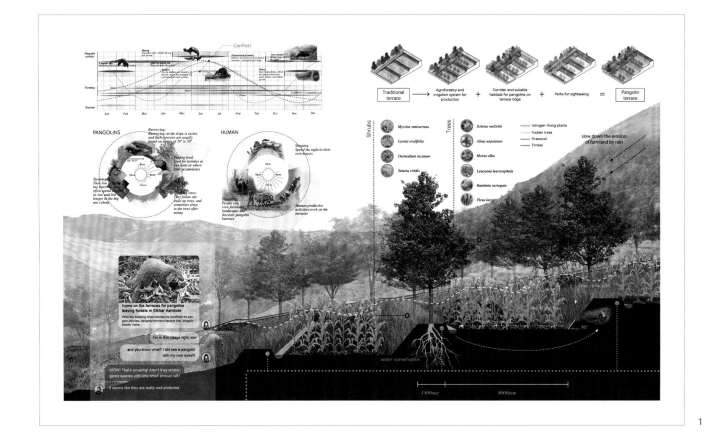

1 Yi Lu + Ruomin Jiang: Chinese pangolin habitat replete with termites is designed into rice terraces so that this much exploited animal, fast running out of its natural habitat, can coexist with humans.

2 Yunge Lei + Yingying Zhao: A landscape corridor for the safe migration of African elephants in Botswana.

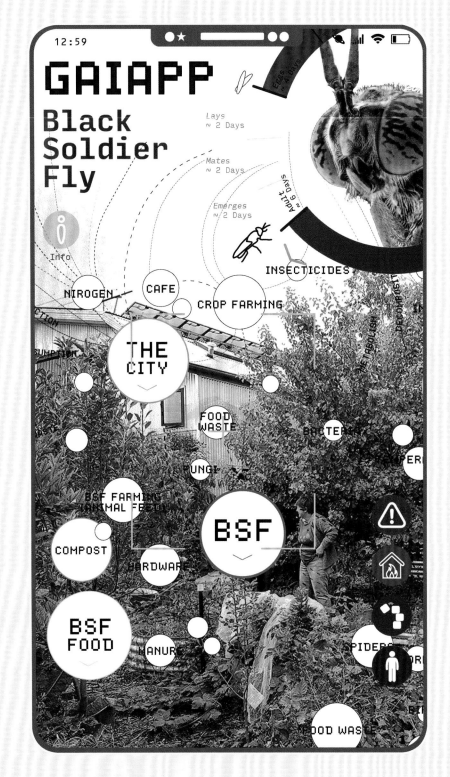

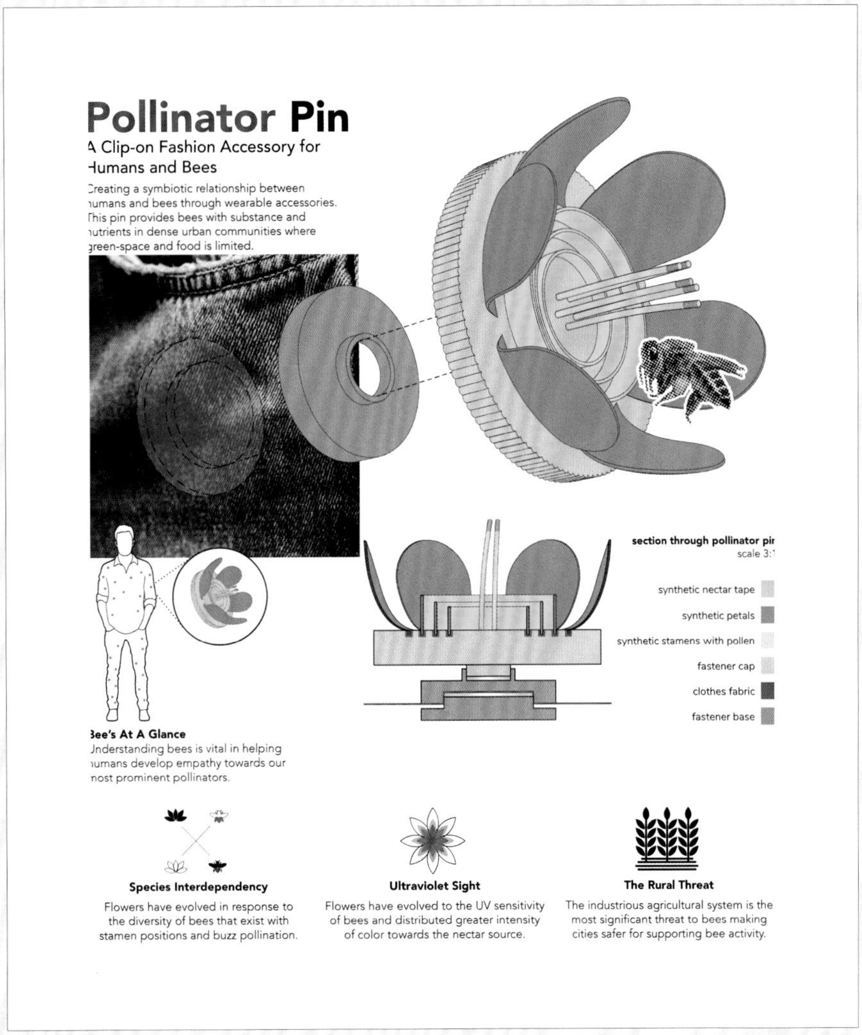

Pollinator Pin

A Clip-on Fashion Accessory for Humans and Bees

Creating a symbiotic relationship between humans and bees through wearable accessories. This pin provides bees with substance and nutrients in dense urban communities where green-space and food is limited.

section through pollinator pin
scale 3:1

synthetic nectar tape
synthetic petals
synthetic stamens with pollen
fastener cap
clothes fabric
fastener base

Bee's At A Glance

Understanding bees is vital in helping humans develop empathy towards our most prominent pollinators.

Species Interdependency

Flowers have evolved in response to the diversity of bees that exist with stamen positions and buzz pollination.

Ultraviolet Sight

Flowers have evolved to the UV sensitivity of bees and distributed greater intensity of color towards the nectar source.

The Rural Threat

The industrious agricultural system is the most significant threat to bees making cities safer for supporting bee activity.

2

1 Vishnu Hazell + Bede Brennan: Black soldier flies are important to urban ecosystems and serve as avid composters – champions of decay and regeneration. Here, custom-designed compost hubs are installed throughout the city to facilitate the ecosystem services the flies provide.

2 Donna Mena + Sharan Saboji: The pollinator pin is an ultra-violet item of wearable jewelry containing synthetic nectar and pollen for urban bees to harvest.

2

**1 Zaid Kashef Alghata, Tucker van Leuwen-Hall +
Minglu Wei:** The 18th-century etching "Cuccagna
on the Square before the Royal Palace in Naples" is
appropriated to create the "Ha-Haus" – a space for
domestic food animals to live in a symbiotic manner
with the neighboring inhabitants.

2 Song Zhang: Crows supplement their diets by
eating ash. In this proposal the ashes of cremated
bodies are lifted into a tower in a park in London to
supply a group of crows who live in the region and
form a new ritual.

1

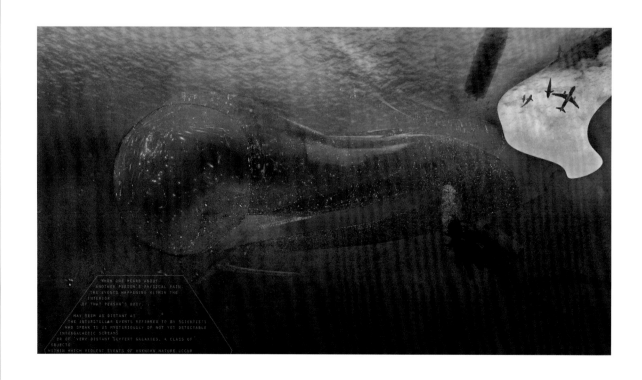

2

3

1 Brent Solomon, Selen Kurt + Eirini Sampani: Bioluminescent marine organisms are farmed and used to light up the urban streetscape and recycled through other industries.

2 James Andrew Billingsley: Cellulose, iron filings, and enzymes are added to the ocean to create blooms of pyrosomes, which form large gelatinous "windows" that break the surface of the ocean and allow the human eye to see into the water.

3 Charlotte Beaudon-Römer + Stepan Nest: An experimental instrument designed to efface the boundary between humans and fly maggots.

1 Karissa Campos, Yoni Carnice + Jena Tegeler: Groves of fruit trees are established across and Thai city of Lopburi in order to decentralize, sustain, and integrate the long-tailed macaque monkey population into the daily life of the city.

2 Melita Schmeckpeper: A program of pigeon coops for school rooftops in dense urban areas serve as catalysts for education, interaction, and community engagement.

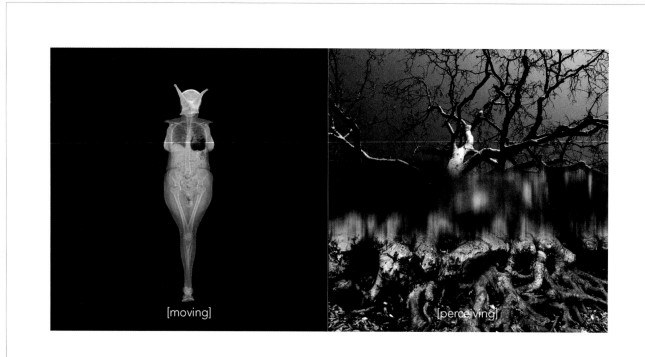

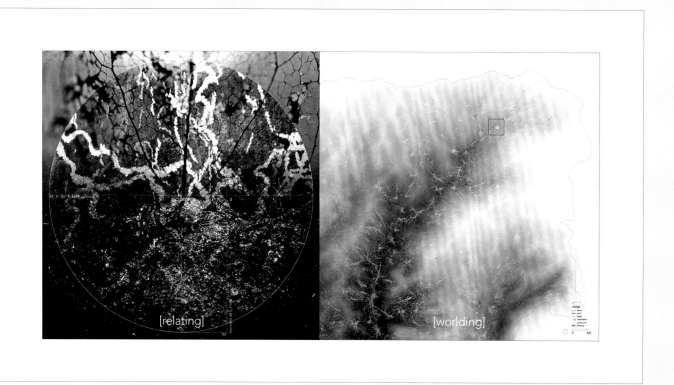

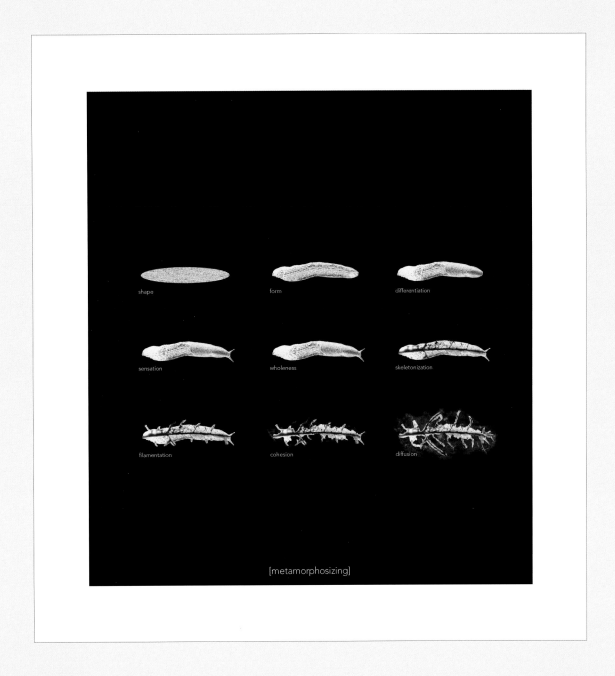

Xan Lillehei: A large concrete slab is designed as a platform for humans but in that platform, cracks appear. In these cracks happily live slugs, a remarkable but easily overlooked creature.

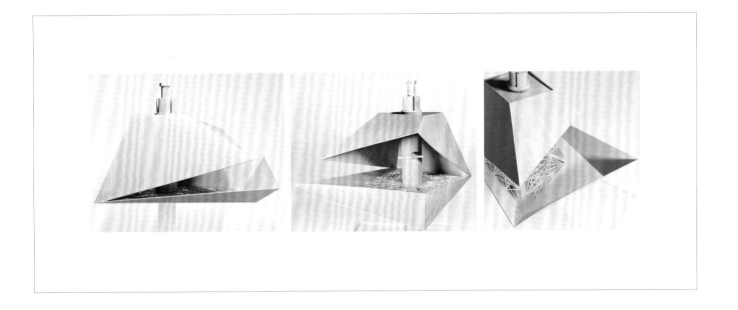

Xu Lian, Yifan Feng + Yanhao Chai: Nest poles derived from the design of traditional Chinese architectural eaves, which Beijing swifts like but are increasingly precluded from nesting in, are distributed throughout the city of Beijing.

2

1 **Chang Huai-Yan, Goh Yu Han + Liew Hann Sheng:** A rooftop garden adjacent to a gene-splicing laboratory designed to incubate the many mosquito species that do not prey on humans and which are otherwise being eradicated by our efforts to kill the ones that do.

2 **Jacky Bowring:** A practical kit of parts for people to remove and bury creatures killed on roads and to tag the place of death with stenciled outlines.

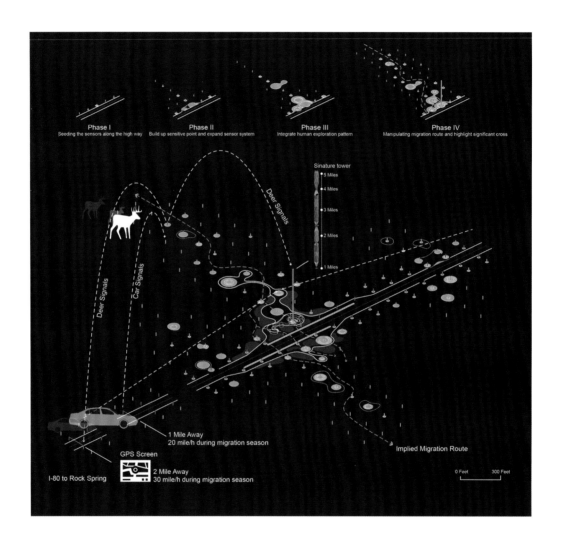

1 Wanlin Zhang: Instead of building expensive overpasses for wild animals that reinforce an "us and them" mentality, this proposal deploys a signaling system at locations where known mule deer migration routes intersect with roads.

2 Selina Cheah + Elliot M. Bullen: A rumination on the symbolic meanings of carp in China with a focus on their scarcity in the Yangtze river and their status elsewhere as invasive species.

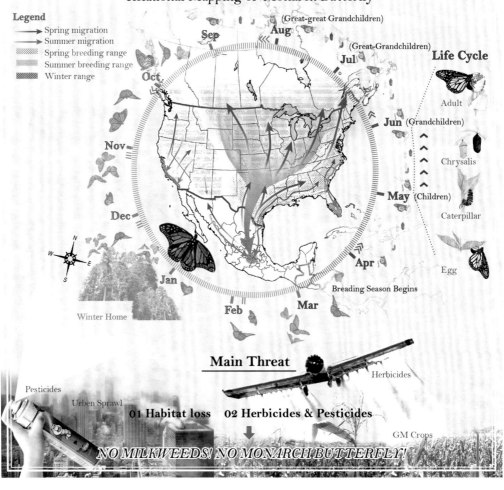

Section/Perspective: Ersatz Forest

0'   4'

2

1 Jingyi Zhou, Shuzhen Gao + Xiao Tan: A transnational network of communities and landscapes devoted to supporting the monarch butterfly to make its epic annual migration from Mexico to Canada.

2 Madeleine Ghillany-Lehar + Rohan Lewis: Textured shade structures encourage lichen growth for woodland caribou in logged old-growth forests.

THE SNAIL TRAIL EST. 2020
FRESNO COUNTY, CA

1

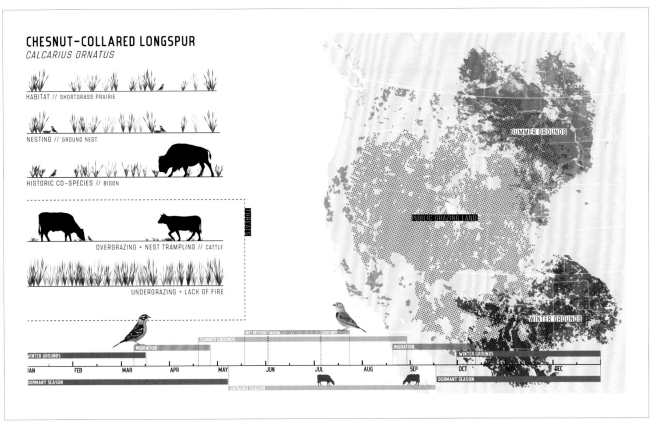

CHESNUT-COLLARED LONGSPUR
CALCARIUS ORNATUS

HABITAT // SHORTGRASS PRAIRIE

NESTING // GROUND NEST

HISTORIC CO-SPECIES // BISON

OVERGRAZING + NEST TRAMPLING // CATTLE

UNDERGRAZING + LACK OF FIRE

SUMMER GROUNDS

PUBLIC GRAZING LAND

WINTER GROUNDS

WINTER GROUNDS
MIGRATION
SUMMER GROUNDS
MIGRATION
WINTER GROUNDS

JAN   FEB   MAR   APR   MAY   JUN   JUL   AUG   SEP   OCT   NOV   DEC

DORMANT SEASON
GROWING SEASON
DORMANT SEASON

2

1 Jayson Latady: A revegetated "snail trail" wends its way through the citrus monoculture of California providing preferable snail habitat to keep snails from damaging crops, while also providing a recreational amenity for humans.

2 Emily Knox: Partnerships between ranchers, cattle, and longspur birds using fire and grazing regimes serve to rebuild a more complex ecology in denuded range lands.

American Cliff Swallow
Petrochelidon pyrrhonota

Acjachemen peoples
'Juaneño'

2

1 Samuel Ridge: A story of the relationship and potential for future decolonized coexistence between the American Cliff swallow and the Acjachemen peoples of San Juan.

2 Diego García Rodríguez: A new zodiac based on zooplankton to foster relationships between humanity and organisms now recognized as fundamental to the function of the Earth system.

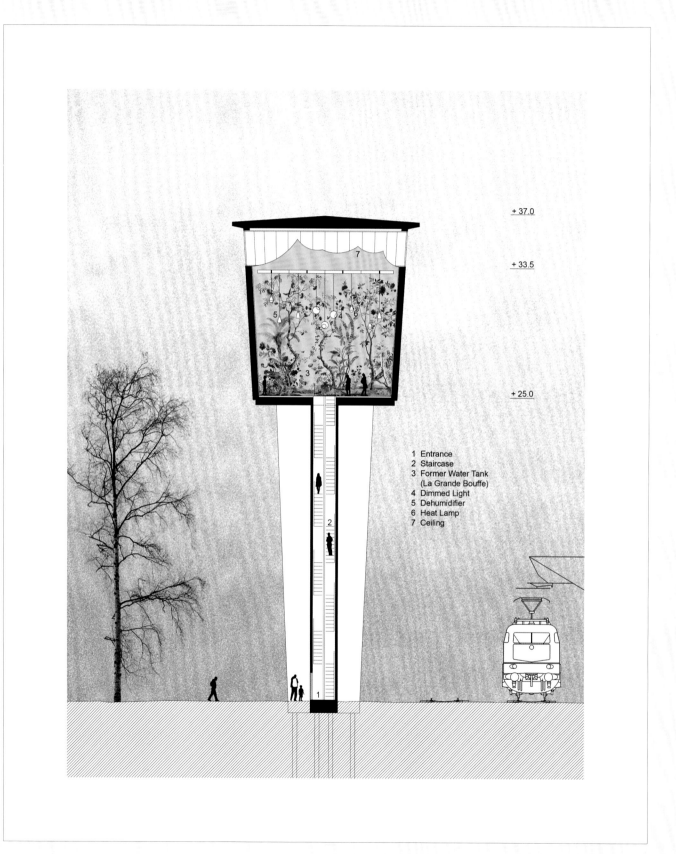

1 Entrance
2 Staircase
3 Former Water Tank
 (La Grande Bouffe)
4 Dimmed Light
5 Dehumidifier
6 Heat Lamp
7 Ceiling

+ 37.0

+ 33.5

+ 25.0

Floor Plan 1:200

Section 1:200

Detail 2:1

1 Skirting Board
2 Egg Deposition
3 Cruising Ground
4 Snippet Storage
5 Moulting Area
6 Wallpaper

15mm

EDITOR'S CHOICE

Sophie Panzer: As our libraries and archives increasingly move toward the digital, the habitats and food sources of the paper silverfish become threatened. In this proposal, the interior of an abandoned water tower in Hamburg, Germany is wallpapered and repurposed as an "eatery" for paper silverfish, as well as providing optimal conditions of humidity and temperature for breeding. A narrow staircase at the foot of the water tower leads visitors to the main room where, surrounded by a colorful jungle of slowly decaying wallpaper, they will witness the entropic beauty of this grand feast.

LA+

In the middle of the electromagnetic spectrum between the binary extremes of black and white it's not gray, as you might expect, but green. And within green's bandwidth there are more tonal variations than any other color can make. Maybe this is why—envy, naivete, and money aside—green is generally synonymous with good. Green is paradise for Islam, luck for the Irish, and a healthy planet for environmentalists. Whereas the industrial past was gray, the future is green. **LA+ GREEN** explores the green spectrum from plants to politics and from art to science, with contributions from:

OUT **SPRING 2022**

NOAM CHOMSKY

ROBERT D. BULLARD

KASSIA ST. CLAIR

NEIL MAHER

ROB LEVINTHAL

SONJA DÜMPELMANN

PEDER ANKER

ROBERT MCDONALD

PARKER SUTTON

DANIEL BARBER

NICHOLAS PEVZNER

MICHAEL MARDER

SHANNON MATTERN

JULIAN BOLLETER

RICHARD WELLER

MICHAEL GEFFEL

BRIAN OSBORN

JULIAN RAXWORTHY

WILD SPRING 2015	PLEASURE FALL 2015	TYRANNY SPRING 2016
SIMULATION FALL 2016	IDENTITY SPRING 2017	RISK FALL 2017
IMAGINATION SPRING 2018	TIME FALL 2018	DESIGN SPRING 2019

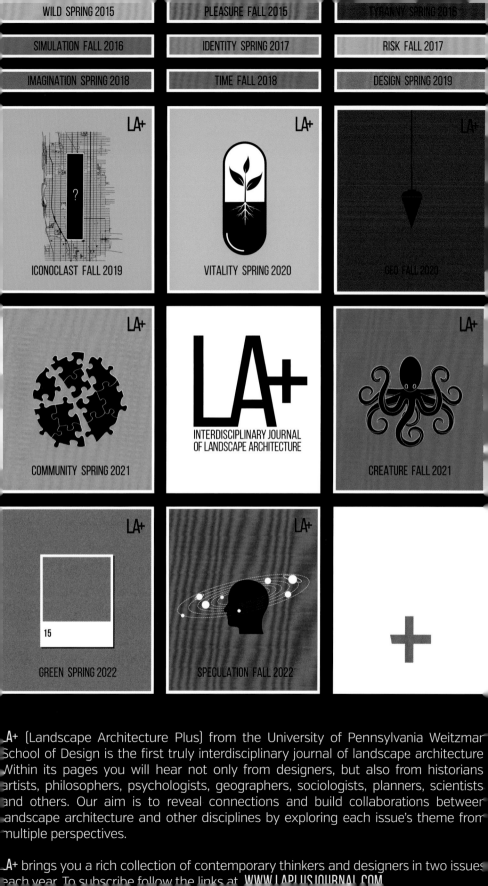

ICONOCLAST FALL 2019	VITALITY SPRING 2020	GEO FALL 2020
COMMUNITY SPRING 2021	LA+ INTERDISCIPLINARY JOURNAL OF LANDSCAPE ARCHITECTURE	CREATURE FALL 2021
GREEN SPRING 2022	SPECULATION FALL 2022	

LA+ (Landscape Architecture Plus) from the University of Pennsylvania Weitzman School of Design is the first truly interdisciplinary journal of landscape architecture. Within its pages you will hear not only from designers, but also from historians, artists, philosophers, psychologists, geographers, sociologists, planners, scientists and others. Our aim is to reveal connections and build collaborations between landscape architecture and other disciplines by exploring each issue's theme from multiple perspectives.

LA+ brings you a rich collection of contemporary thinkers and designers in two issues each year. To subscribe follow the links at WWW.LAPLUSJOURNAL.COM